Interface Theology:
Volume 1, Number 2, 2015

Editorial Manager
Mr Hilary Regan, Publisher, ATF Theology, PO Box 504 Hindmarsh. SA 5007, Australia. Fax +61 8 82235643.

Subscription rates
Print: Local: Individual Aus $55, Institutions Aus $65.
Overseas: Individuals US $60, Institutions US $65.

Interface Theology is a biannual refereed journal of theology published in print, epub and open access by ATF Press in Australia.
The journal is a scholarly ecumenical and interdisciplinary publication, aiming to serve the church and its mission, promoting a broad based interpretation of Christian theology within a trinitarian context, encouraging dialogue between Christianity and other faiths, and exploring the interface between faith and culture. It is published in English for an international audience.

ISSN 2203-465X
Cover design by Astrid Sengkey. Text Minion Pro Size 11

An imprint of ATF Theology part of the ATF Press Publishing Group.
ATF (Australia) Ltd.
PO Box 504
Hindmarsh SA 5007
Australia
www.atfpress.com
Making a lasting impact

Economic and Ecotheological Responses to *Laudato Si'*

Table of Contents

Editorial

Laudato Si' is a call for 'conversion from exploitation to love'.[1] It addresses all of humanity, and Christians in particular, with the value, future, potential, and current problems of creation.

This edition of *Interface Theology* addresses *Laudato Si'* through a number of lenses. At 45,000 words, *Laudato Si'* weighs in heavily. Its rich thematic engagement qualifies it as a heavy duty piece of theology. The responses it has generated, from religious and other sources, has shown that it is hard-hitting.

Norman Habel and Marie Turner both use the lens of scripture and biblical interpretation. Habel interrogates the use of biblical language and passages to support Pope Francis' 'appeal for a new dialogue about how we are shaping the future of our planet'. Beyond proof-texting, though sometime using scripture as a bridge to talk eco-theologically, Turner notes that Pope Francis is 'attuned to contemporary biblical scholarship'. Habel notes that the groaning of creation may be travail or hope—or both. Thus past and present are connected to God in creation. Habel points to some failures to engage with potentially useful texts, such as Job 8, in supporting the call to ecological conversion and the practice of ecological spirituality. Turner concurs. The potential of 'a much richer ecotheology' is unrealised. Yet, 'true to his papal namesake, St Francis of Assisi, Pope Francis allows his delight in the wonders of God's creation. . . to shine through this document.'

Abigail Lofte brings the lens of eschatological christology to *Laudato Si'*. As a call to 'responsible action founded on wonder and awe of the universe' the encyclical would have yet more power, she argues, had it drawn more explicitly on the resurrection of Christ. This en-

---

1. Andy Hamilton, 'Why Pope Francis' new encyclical is so radical' *Eureka Street*, 25/12 (online at http://www.eurekastreet.com.au/article.aspx?aeid=4378).

gagement would strengthen the urgency of the encyclical's call to an ecological mission based on eschatological hope as a participation in the ongoing life of Christ in the world.

Pope Francis' call for mutual respect between theology and science has received substantial public attention. Ted Peters uses this binocular vision to examine *Laudato Si'*, noting that the theological lens of the encyclical is focussed on repentance. Thus the pope 'demonstrates by example the dynamics of partnership between science and moral resolve'. With Lofte, Peters laments the lack of an eschatological focus, for him enhanced through a 'treatment of God's promise of a new creation'.

Frank Brennan brings three questions to the encyclical: Why would Pope Francis write to everyone; Why have something to say about climate change; What new ideas are contained in the letter? To the first, Brennan notes the inclusivity of the pontiff and his ability to speak beyond 'Vaticanese' to universal human concerns. To the second, the encyclical builds on a real and urgent concern, a perceived lack of leadership on the issue, and an unwillingness to trust governments or the market alone. Conceding that 'there are probably no genuinely new ideas in the encyclical', Brennan notes its folksy style as part of its impact.

Bruce Duncan takes issue with the trenchant criticism of the encyclical in the Murdoch Press's *The Australian* newspaper. Duncan shows how *Laudato Si'* with other recent encyclicals critiques unbridled capitalism as a system and greed as a personal rule. The perpetuation of poverty and hunger are moral issues that need to be addressed.

Peter Hess brings the lens of concern about overpopulation to the encyclical and the lack of attention given to this in *Laudato Si'*. Whilst the church lives out care for the poor, it fails to address one contributing factor, overpopulation. This, says Hess, is an issue of ecclesiology, not simply eschatology. Human induced climate change cannot be listed as an issue of concern if population control is not a factor considered in its remediation. Nevertheless, *Laudato Si'* is 'a good first foray by Catholic Church leadership into discussions of ecological degradation'.

The eighth and final essay brings the lens of death to the encyclical, noting the absence of any sustained discussion and the omission of the verse of the hymn which Francis added as his own death approached: 'Be praised my Lord through our Sister Bodily Death'. Anthony Kelly introduces consideration of 'integral ecology' and the reality that lament accompanies hope, as death accompanies life.

The rich refraction of the splendour of *Laudato Si'* in this volume invites a richer exploration of themes present in the encyclical and those absent. As the encyclical itself says (#16, emphasis added):

> . . . a number of themes. . . reappear as the Encyclical unfolds. . . the **intimate relationship between the poor and the fragility of the planet,** the **conviction that everything in the world is connected,** the **critique of new paradigms and forms of power derived from technology,** the **call to seek other ways of understanding the economy and progress,** the **value proper to each creature,** the **human meaning of ecology,** the **need for forthright and honest debate,** the **serious responsibility of international and local policy,** the **throwaway culture** and the **proposal of a new lifestyle.** These questions will not be dealt with once and for all, but reframed and enriched again and again.

These essays have addressed many of the items highlighted and invite further reframing and enrichment through 'forthright and honest debate'.

Three remarkable elements stand out to me in the encyclical: as a human being, the address to the whole of humanity; as a non-Catholic, the warm inclusion of Patriarch Bartholomew and other non-Catholics; as a theologian, the reference to (and clear dependence in parts on) Romano Guardini, and a footnote referring to Pierre Teilhard de Chardin.

I noted only one passing reference to disability. Given that all humans are afflicted by and called forth to the travail of creation, disability is a reality of life, and has grown in its prevalence in recent theological discourse. Is *Laudato Si'* to be condemned by this lack? I think not. The richness of the encyclical means that it can inspire further thinking and reflection. In our frailness we find true hope and deeper potential.

It is the hope of the editorial board that this collection of essays will contribute to our care for our common home, as an act of joyful obedience, in communion with our children and our Lord. We express our thanks to Hilary Regan for his work in identifying, gathering and preparing such a splendid international and interdisciplinary set of papers.

John Capper
Melbourne

The Biblical in the Encyclical Bible Interpretations and *Laudato Si'*

Norman Habel

Introduction

The encyclical *Laudato Si'* is a powerful document, rich in theological, social, ecological, environmental and biblical insights. My study will focus on the use and reading of the biblical passages cited to support Pope Francis' 'appeal for a new dialogue about how we are shaping the future of our planet.'

The Groaning of Creation

The introduction to the encyclical draws our attention to Romans 8:22 which refers to creation 'groaning in travail.' The encyclical reads this text as an allusion to the way Earth has been abused, laid waste and maltreated by humans. As a result Earth 'groans in travail'. The suffering of the planet is outlined in detail in subsequent chapters of the encyclical.

A close reading of Romans 8, however, reveals that the groans of creation in this passage result from the fact that 'creation was subjected to futility, not willingly, but because of him who subjected it in hope' (8:20). God is the source of this 'curse on creation,' yet creation is depicted as having a voice, 'going into labour and groaning in labour pains,' awaiting a new creation. According to Sigve Tonstad, Romans 8:19–22 invites 'an ecological hermeneutic, speaking explicitly in support of the eco-justice principles of interconnectedness, voice and purpose'.[1] (1)

---

1. Sigve Tonstad, 'Creation Groaning in Labour Pains' in Norman Habel & Perter Trudinger, *Exploring Ecological Hermeneutics* (Leiden: Brill, 2008), 141–150.

In this Romans passage, creation, humans and the Spirit cooperate with God in anticipation of Earth's redemption. According to the ecological reading of Brendan Byrne in *The Earth Bible Volume One*, 'creation's groaning is a positive aspiration . . . an index of hope.'[2] The curse that causes Earth's groaning precedes the current abuse of our planet, but in ecological terms the past and the present are inter-related and the labour pains of Earth are both past and present.

There are, moreover, a number of passages, especially in the prophets, where domains of creation have a voice, groaning or crying out because of human abuse.[3] According to Jeremiah 12:10–11, God's vineyard has become desolate and 'mourns to me' (cf 4:28; 23:10). In the plagues that the prophet Joel describes, the 'beasts groan' and the 'wild beasts cry out' to God. These references to the groaning by domains of creation also emphasise that the groaning creation has a voice that needs to be heard in the current environmental crisis.

God's Presence in Creation

The Introduction to the encyclical, citing Saint Francis as 'faithful to Scripture,' refers to creation as the book of nature through which God's infinite beauty and goodness are 'glimpsed' as indicated in Wisdom of Solomon 13:5. Even more specific is Romans 1:20, where Paul maintains that, 'God's eternal power and divinity have been made known through his works ever since the creation of the world. Following Saint Francis, the encyclical interprets these two texts as witnesses to the living presence of God in creation.

Just as significant in this connection is Isaiah 6:3, a text which deserves to be included in the encyclical. In this text, the seraphim declare that 'the whole Earth is *filled* with the presence of God (*kabod YHWH*)'. In the wilderness, the tabernacle was once been *filled* with that same divine 'presence.'[4] This revelation is consistent with the

---

2. Brendan Byrne SJ, 'Creation Groaning: An Earth Bible Reading of Romans 8:18–22' in *Readings from the Perspective of Earth, The Earth Bible Volume One* (Sheffield: Sheffield Academic Press, 2000), 193–203.

3. Note the analysis of Katherine Hayes who discovers the 'mourning' of Earth in Amos, Hosea, Jeremiah, Isaiah and Joel. Katherine Hayes, *'The Earth Mourns' Prophetic Metaphor and Oral Aesthetic* (Atlanta: SBL, 2002).

4. For a more detailed analysis of Presence in creation see Norman Habel, *Rainbow of Mysteries. Meeting the Sacred in Nature* (Kelowna: Woodlake, 2012), 34–38.

claim of Martin Luther that God's presence is 'in, with and under everything' in creation.

Later, in chapter two, the encyclical pursues this line and claims that 'the entire material universe speaks of God's love, his boundless affection for us'. Nature is described as a 'continuing revelation of the divine.' The encyclical also cites the Bishops of Brazil who declare that 'nature as a whole not only manifests God but is also a locus of his presence.'

This leads me to ask precisely what is intended by the expression *The Gospel of Creation* which is the title of chapter two. Does the expression refer to the Good News that God's presence, power and compassion are revealed through creation as indicated in these passages, or does it refer to the message that the cosmic Christ is the medium through whom God was pleased to reconcile himself to all things (Col 1:19–20), 'all things' being a reference to all creation. In this context, it may well be worth comparing this chapter title to the memory of Jesus commissioning his disciples to 'preach the Gospel *to* the whole creation' (Mk 16:15), rather than discern the Gospel *in* or *of* creation.

God's Commissions in Genesis 1 and 2

The texts of Genesis 1 and 2 include two discrete commissions by God in relationship to Earth and the creatures of Earth. The first is the commission to 'subdue' Earth and have 'dominion over' living creatures (Gen 1:26–28). The second is the commission to 'serve' and 'preserve' the domain called Eden (Gen 2:15).

The introduction to the encyclical refers to the creation of the first man (Gen 2:7) as significant. While the original narrative of Genesis 2 is a primal myth about the first human being moulded from clay by a divine potter,[5] an ecological approach focuses on the clay or dust which is the substance of the moulding of the first mortal and links it to the reality that 'our very bodies are made of her (Earth's) elements including air and waters'. The significance of this reading by the encyclical is that it highlights the role of Earth as mother and human beings as children of Earth who ought to take care of their mother.

---

5. Norman Habel, *The Birth, the Curse and the Greening of Earth, An Ecological Reading of Genesis 1–11. The Earth Bible Commentary, Volume 1* (Sheffield: Sheffield Phoenix, 2011), chapter 4.

In this passage, the Bible is consistent with the science of ecology in recognising that humans are moulded in the womb of Mother Earth (See also Ps 139:13–15).

Perhaps the most controversial text in this area is the commission associated with the *imago dei* in Genesis 1:26–28 and sometimes designated 'the mandate to dominate'. Saint John Paul II may have stated that the 'special love of the Creator for each human being confers on him or her an infinite dignity'. The text as such, however, remains problematic. Humans, made in the image of God are commissioned to 'fill the Earth and subdue it' and to 'have dominion over all living creatures' (Gen 1:28). Crucial in the reading of this text is that the verb 'have dominion' in Hebrew (*rada*) means to 'rule as a monarch' while the verb 'subdue' (*kabash*) refers to crushing and even the rape of women.[6] Understandably this text has been cited to justify human harnessing and domination of nature.

When we re-consider the text of Genesis 2:15 we uncover a diametrically different perspective. Humans are commissioned to 'serve and preserve' Eden. The respective verbs used in these two commission texts are antonyms:

> rule (*rada*) is the opposite of serve (*abad*) and
> subdue (*kabash*) is the opposite of preserve (*shamar*).

These two commission texts from Genesis One and Genesis Two reflect two different ways of portraying the relationship of humans to Earth. It is helpful here to turn to Mark 10:42–45 where Jesus clearly links us with the second text when he urges his disciples to be 'servants' of all, rather than 'rulers' like those who rule among the Gentiles. Here Jesus provides us with an 'appropriate hermeneutic' with ecological dimensions and validates the Genesis 2 text.

There is a further reference to Genesis 2:15 in Chapter three of the encyclical where the primal pair are commissioned to care for the primordial garden, which upon close analysis is a forest filled with trees of great diversity and beauty. The full force of this text is apparent when we recognise that the verb translated 'till' normally means 'serve', the opposite of the verb for 'rule' found in Genesis 1:28,

---

6. For a detailed comparison of these two commissions see Norman Habel, *An Inconvenient Text. Is a Green Reading of the Bible Possible?* (Adelaide: ATF Press, 2009), chapter 1 & 6.

while the verb rendered 'keep' also means to 'preserve'. This primordial commission, then, is a mandate, not to 'subdue' but to 'preserve' the forests of planet Earth, the Eden of our generation.

God's Covenant with Creation

In its discussion about the Flood, the encyclical highlights that Earth had become filled with violence (Gen 6:13) and that God was sorry 'he had made man on Earth' (Gen 6:6). What has been omitted, however, is the decision of God to destroy Earth along with all living creatures (Gen 6:13). The God who created Earth was ready to destroy Earth, a rather harsh decision. In the end, however, God repents and representatives of all life are preserved.

Especially relevant is the rainbow symbol which appears after the Flood. The Creator not only promises never to send another flood to destroy Earth and life on Earth (Gen 6:15), but also makes 'a covenant with Earth' (Gen 6:13). The rainbow is the sign of a personal bond or partnership with Earth, a covenant promise that God will protect the planet and ultimately all creation.

The relevance of another passage (Ps 136:6) cited in this connection deserves further attention. In relation to each of the divine acts of creation cited in this Psalm, including the spreading of waters over Earth, God's *chesed* is present. This *chesed* is the 'covenant love' and compassion of the Creator, and recalls the personal covenant made with Earth after the Flood. Also relevant is Psalm 33 in which another Psalmist declares that 'the whole Earth is filled with the *chesed* of the God' who creates the skies by the divine word (Ps 33:9–10). This recalls an earlier reference (Isa 6:3), in which Earth is not only 'filled' with God's presence (*kabod*) but is also 'filled' with the Creator's covenant compassion (*chesed*).

Celebrating with Creation

Also important in this context are passages where all creatures and domains of creation are summoned to praise the Creator (for example, Ps 96 and Ps 148). All domains of cosmos are capable of praising God. They are not only rejuvenated by the Spirit of God (Ps 104:30), but also inspired to praise their Creator. The Creator Spirit is also the sustaining Spirit permeating creation.

The encyclical, following the insights of ecology, argues from the Catechism, that 'God wills the inter-dependence of creatures . . .

the sun, the moon, the cedar, the flower, the sparrow and the eagle.' 'Creatures exist only in dependence on each other' and praise their Creator in unison. It is perhaps relevant at this point to refer to *The Season of Creation* which celebrates a three year cycle of praise-based biblical texts linked with creation.[7] In *The Season of Creation*, the worshipper not only gives thanks *for* creation but also worships *with* creation.

The encyclical also cites texts that indicate that humans should obey the laws of nature, including the Sabbath laws (for example, Ex 23:12), recognise that 'all creatures have a value of their own in God's eyes' and that 'the Lord rejoices in all his works' (Ps 104:31). The Creator, it seems, also celebrates the wonders of creation. These texts are consistent with an ecology which recognises the intrinsic value of all creatures who are our kin and children of Mother Earth.

The Cosmic Christ

The closing section of Chapter Two is entitled 'The Gaze of Jesus' and cites a range of texts reflecting Jesus' relationship to creation and the profound mystery of the cosmic Christ. Jesus' sermons include affirmations about how God cares personally for all creatures, whether they be sparrows or other birds of the air (Mt 6:26; Lk 12:6). Jesus' harmony with creation is revealed in his stilling of the storm when 'even the winds and the waves of the sea obey him' (Mt 8:27). It is significant that the encyclical interprets Jesus' actions as reflecting a harmony with creation that is far removed from the unhealthy dualisms or world views that 'despise the body, matter and the things of this world.' This suggests that Jesus' words and actions are interpreted here as being consistent with a harmonious ecological interrelationship between the spiritual and the material.

The chapter closes with a brief consideration of John 1:1–18, Colossians 1:16, 19–20 and 1 Corinthians 15:28, passages which I would have thought were worthy of more intensive ecological analysis. The ecological implications of the Word becoming the very 'flesh' that all living creatures possess deserves further attention. The presence of God permeating creation is celebrated earlier in the chapter, but

---

7. For the ecumenical worship materials related to *The Season of Creation* see www.seasonofcreation.com. Recently a Catholic version of *The Season of Creation* has been developed by the Columbian Mission Institute in Sydney.

the possibility that 'flowers of the field' are 'imbued with the radiant presence of the risen Christ' does not seem to be evident from the passages cited. According to the encyclical, the cosmic Christ is apparently revealed through the beauty of nature.

Ecological Conversion

Chapter four provides a significant analysis of the many dimensions of ecology—cultural, biological, social, human—and how they may be interpreted in terms of an integral ecology. While integral ecology is viewed as the work of the Creator, no biblical passages are cited in connection with this analysis. Likewise, in Chapter five where lines of approach to confront the current environmental crisis are explored, no biblical passages are cited to support the arguments for specific actions.

In the closing chapter which explores ecological spirituality, we might expect a range of relevant biblical texts to be cited. Especially significant is the call for 'ecological conversion whereby the effects of our encounter with Jesus Christ become evident in our relationship with the world around us'. This conversion is seen as important for 'achieving reconciliation with creation' a goal that echoes God's reconciliation with 'all things' (Col 1:19–20) achieved for us through Christ, a passage not cited in this context. Ecological conversion, it is argued, can 'inspire us to resolve the world's problems by offering ourselves to God' as 'a living sacrifice, holy and acceptable' (Rom 12:1). While Romans 12 does not specifically consider human relationships with nature, the orientation recommended is appropriate.

A biblical example of ecological conversion ignored in the encyclical, but which deserves special consideration, is found in the Book of Job.[8] In the course of the narrative, Job moves from being totally anthropocentric to being ecologically conscious and spiritually rejuvenated. Throughout his dialogue with his friends, Job is asking 'where can justice be found for me?' He even challenges God to appear in court to handle Job's case. Midway through the narrative the poet asks the pivotal question, 'Where can wisdom be found?' When God answers in Job 38, God takes Job on a tour of the cosmos, challenging his understanding of the laws and inter-related domains of

---

8. Norman Habel, *Discerning Wisdom in God's Creation. Following the Way of Ancient Scientists* (Melbourne: Morning Star, 2015), chapter 5 and pages 64–66.

creation that are governed by innate Wisdom. Job experiences what might be called an ecological conversion and announces that he has discerned/seen God in the cosmos (42:5) by virtue of his intense interaction with the interrelated forces and mysteries of creation.

Conclusion

The encyclical focuses on the environmental background, ecological insights, traditional theologies and relevant approaches for Christians to become relevant agents of change in the face of an environmental crisis. In that context, on the one hand,

a) portions of biblical texts are cited to support the position taken in only a relatively few of the areas under discussion,
b) there is no detailed exegesis of extremely relevant texts such as Genesis 2 or Colossians 1,
c) ecological hermeneutics are not explicitly employed as an interpretive strategy for identifying relevant biblical insights.[9]

On the other hand, this encyclical,

a) is a powerful call to action in the face of multiple forces that degrade creation, and recognises key passages in the Bible as grounds for such a call,
b) dares to identify the book of nature and the Gospel of creation as sources of revelation parallel with biblical texts in the exploration of the spiritual that is relevant in the current crisis,
c) embraces the science of ecology as a partner with the Bible as a means of educating the Christian community to take action.

---

9.   The principles of ecological hermeneutics are outlined in Norman Habel & Peter Trudinger, *Exploring Ecological Hermeneutics* (Leiden: Brill, 2008), 1–8.

Pope Francis' Use of Scripture in *Laudato Si'*

Marie Turner

In his encyclical *Laudato Si'*, Pope Francis has broken new ground in more ways than one. Pope John Paul II had already drawn to our attention the need for ecological conversion in *Evangelium Vitae* (2001),

> It is the ecological question–ranging from the preservation of the nat-ural habitats of the different species of animals and of other forms of life to 'human ecology' properly speaking—which finds in the Bible clear and strong ethical direction, leading to a solution which respects the great good of life, of every life (*EV* 42).

Laudato Si', however, is the first encyclical which has been entirely devoted to the issue of the environmental crisis facing 'our common home'. Refreshingly, this encyclical does not unequivocally approach the Scriptural underpinning of our responsibility from 'proof-texting', as is often the way of encyclicals. Proof-texting is an approach to a theological question in which the writer begins from an *a priori* posi-tion, and then supports the position with a generally apt biblical verse. This is not the usual approach of Pope Francis in *Laudato Si'*. His prac-tice is rather to move more often from a Scripture text to an eco-theo-logical position. This is not to say that he never uses proof-texting, or that he sets out to exegete the biblical text as though he were doing a full-blown interpretation of scripture; but it does mean that for the most part, he is attuned to contemporary biblical scholarship, and the field of biblical scholarship has much in common with his approach in this encyclical. In these ways, then, the encyclical has much to say to a contemporary audience particularly interested in the interface between pertinent biblical texts and ecological issues.

The encyclical does not move immediately into an exploration of biblical texts. Pope Francis turns first to St Francis, a figure dear to his heart and whom he has chosen as a guide and inspiration for his role as Bishop of Rome. The first Scripture text he calls upon to set the biblical scene, as it were, for his deliberations, is Romans 8:22, the 'groaning of creation' text. The pope uses the 'groaning of creation' as symbolic of the environmental crisis, connecting the cry of the earth and the cry of the poor (2). While there is a slight tendency here towards proof-texting, it would be quibbling to criticise this approach here, in light of the figurative and poetic nature of the text. In its original context St Paul probably had in mind the sin and death which came into the world through Adam, and so the pope has actually moved straight to a contemporary ecological hermeneutic, connecting the text to the current environmental crisis. In its biblical context the imagery is used by Paul for a theology of the interconnectedness of all creation in the Spirit of God. The text poetically depicts a positive relationship between humankind for whose liberation from decay creation groans in 'labour pains', humankind itself, groaning as it awaits redemption, and the Spirit who intercedes for us with 'unutterable groanings' (literal meaning of the Greek original). While this could have given rise to a much richer eco-theology, of course it is unrealistic to expect the pope to exegete the text in detail, especially here in an introductory section. Rather, to focus on the interrelationship between humankind and non-human creation, Pope Francis turns to another text, that of Genesis 2:7, to remind us that we are made up of the very dust of the earth and its elements.

In a strikingly inclusive move, Francis names his intended audience as mainly Christians and other believers, but the world at large is in his sights. In keeping with his reference in the subtitle of his encyclical to 'our common home', he hopes that 'the whole human family' will come together in the ecological task that faces us in seeking a sustainable and integral development (13). In a brief overview of his environmental forerunners he refers to several of his papal predecessors and to the Patriarch Bartholomew. He then deals in chapter one with the environmental crisis itself. Here he includes the problems we face, weak responses to the crisis, and some positive improvements.

It is in chapter two entitled 'The Gospel of Creation' that Francis moves directly to the Scripture texts, rather than simply selecting an appropriate example of an already decided position. In a very clear statement of an often misunderstood position, he declares at the outset that there is no conflict between science and religion, and, indeed, 'intense dialogue' is fruitful (62). While this has long been the Roman Catholic position, it is a timely and important reminder to the many who are either oblivious or uninformed of the Church's stance.

He poses a question as the framework within which he examines Scripture: what do the great biblical narratives say about the relationship of human beings with the world? As he rightly points out, he cannot repeat the whole theology of creation (65); but he moves now to the texts of scripture to offer biblical insights into his own question. Francis works from his chosen Scriptures to resolve his ecological position, rather than moving from an already decided *a priori* position to the Scripture; clearly, 'proof-texting' is not his practice.

His exploration of the Scripture texts begins with a cursory look at Genesis 1, with its declaration that God saw that everything God created was good; and that men and women were created out of love in the image and likeness of God (1:26). He parallels this theological concept with Jeremiah 1:5 'Before I formed you in the womb I knew you, and before you were born I consecrated you; I appointed you a prophet to the nations' (64). In the next paragraph the Pope moves on to Genesis 2. When dealing with these creation texts of Genesis, there is no tendency towards a fundamentalist reading; rather, the pope acknowledges the symbolic and narrative language of Genesis. He identifies the sin of Eden as humanity's presumption of taking the place of God and 'refusing to acknowledge our creaturely limitations' (66). Thus, he avoids the pitfall of a more conventional reading of the text as dealing with the sin of disobedience, opting instead to focus on one of the prevailing literary themes of Genesis, that is, humankind's limitations precisely as human. While this 'humanity' is not *per se* a negative in Francis' thought, he is acutely and accurately aware that our present situation attests to the fact that humankind has its limitations as regards maintaining the harmonious relationship between itself and the natural world. This conflictual relationship has played itself out in a distortion of the command of Gen 1:28 concerning the apparent directive of God to have dominion on the earth. In an interpretation of this controversial text, 'dominion' has often been emphasised, while the command of Genesis 2:15 to 'till and keep' the garden has been neglected. He might have added that one of the Hebrew words used is indeed to 'serve' the earth. The pope could have differentiated between the theologies of Genesis 1 and 2, since the concept of dominion belongs in the more 'regal' style and content of Genesis 1, while the depiction of the 'hands on' Adam as gardener is the more striking image of Genesis 2. Biblical scholars generally prefer to deal separately with the texts of Genesis 1 and 2, at least in the first instance, and allow them to speak their message from their own unique perspective. This kind of detailed comparison between the two texts, however, could not be expected in a document such as this where an extensive exegesis is not the aim, neither is it feasible.

The pope seeks to respond to the charge often laid against the Judaeo-Christian tradition because of an 'incorrect interpretation' of the mandate to 'have dominion' over the earth. The pope perhaps 'side-steps' the fact that in the context of the times, to have dominion, and indeed to 'subdue' something (Gen 1:28) was to control the subject in the manner of an ancient ruler, although one who had a responsibility to rule wisely. Instead, he seeks to soften the concept in the interests of encouraging a healthier attitude, in light of contemporary understandings. As he rightly points out, where the text has been used to dominate and abuse nature, this is an incorrect interpretation, taken out of context (67). We have a responsibility to reject 'anthropocentric tyranny' (68). *The Catechism of the Catholic Church*, he reminds us, 'clearly and forcefully criticises a distorted anthropocentrism' (69). He offers a few sentences containing proof-texts from Psalms, Leviticus and Deuteronomy to underpin his reminder of the Sabbath idea that we must take only what is needed for subsistence, for the earth belongs to God and our duty is to protect it for coming generations. Before leaving Genesis, Francis turns to the Cain and Abel and the Noah narratives to focus on the effect that disharmonious relationships have even on the earth; indeed, Abel's blood cries out from the ground (70–71).

The pope uses texts from Deuteronomy and Exodus to affirm the claim that all creatures reflect in their own ways the goodness and wisdom of God. This is a particular attribute of the wisdom literature of the Bible (Wisdom of Solomon 13:5), to which he refers in chapter one: 'for from the beauty and greatness of creation we can know something of God' (12).

While Francis does move to and fro among the biblical texts, for the most part he groups them according to genre or content. He draws frequently from the poetic books, the Psalms and the Wisdom literature. In a succinct paragraph (72) he is able to pinpoint the particular ethos of the psalms, that all creation joins in the praise of God. In dealing with the prophets he reminds us that the God who saves is also the God who creates. The wisdom literature gives a timely reminder that earth is not the property of humanity to do with as humanity wills, but belongs to the creator, who loves everything that exists (89). Indeed, the pope uses these texts to argue for social justice. 'Every *campesino* has the right to possess a reasonable allotment of land' (94). The Jubilee texts of Leviticus 19:9–10, the Sabbath texts of Genesis 2:2–3, Exodus 16:23 and 20:10 are referred to here.

Moving to the New Testament, the pope refers to Jesus' teaching on the fatherhood of God, and refers to 'the paternal relationship' that God has with all God's creatures (96). He chooses the appropriate proof texts of Mathew 6:26, the birds of the air, and Luke 12:6, where God does not forget the sparrows. Jesus' references to the nature parables (Mt 13:31–32) and his sayings referring to the harvest feature in this section. The Pope has an interesting perspective on the miracle of the wind and sea, seeing it as a sign of Jesus' harmony with all creation. While biblical scholarship would often see the nature miracles as signs that Jesus is uniquely the presence of God, reflecting God's creative power, the pope's interpretation is refreshing and pertinent.

Incarnational theology is conjoined with the Colossians hymn of 1:15–20 that 'all things have been created through him and for him' (Col 1:16), combining this with the *logos* incarnational theology of the prologue to John's Gospel. In his reference to Mathew 11:19, we see the pope's appreciation of contemporary theologies of the body, rejecting the 'unhealthy dualisms' (98) which despised matter and 'disfigured the Gospel'. This was not the philosophy of Jesus, he reminds us. It is in his reflections on the New Testament texts that he expounds in detail his deep incarnational eco-theology. On one level, he recounts the way Jesus appreciated the natural world, but then he delves more deeply into the theology of the incarnation and the implications it has for ecology. He refers again to the Colossians hymn which exults in the risen and glorious Christ, present through all of creation because of his universal Lordship. He conjoins this text with the eschatological text of 1 Corinthians 15:8 which looks to the End Time when God will be everything to everything. He moves from that statement to the natural world which will be imbued with the radiant presence of the Risen Christ (100). It is unlikely that both the Colossians text and the Corinthians text come from the pen of Paul, and some years most probably separate them. It is likely that a disciple of St Paul wrote the Letter to the Colossians in Paul's name, a common practice in the ancient world. Herein, therefore, we can see that Pope Francis is not confined to a rigorous methodology of biblical interpretation, but focuses rather on those texts by which he can best expound his biblical eco-theology.

This is not to say that the document is a work of textbook biblical scholarship. Nor does it set out to be. That would not be expected of an encyclical, and neither does Pope Francis lay claim to the mantle of a professional biblical scholar. The document is intended for a wide readership. At the same time, the pope does give an extended interpretation of some biblical texts which emerge then as a sure foundation for his eco-theolgy. Thus, his understanding of the incarnation provides a wonderful exposé of the deep incarnational theology which underpins his ecological concerns.

Proof-texting is not the preferred approach of biblical scholarship, because in this mode the biblical text is treated in a superficial fashion, often with little reference to its context. Pope Francis for the most part, however, manages to avoid the superficiality. It is clear as one reads chapter two of the document that his eco-theology is based upon authentic scriptural reading, cognisant of contemporary biblical interpretation. While the document does not explicitly express it, the discerning reader can detect a familiarity with the biblical interpretation methods informed by the work of the Pontifical Biblical Commission (1993).

As we ponder Pope Francis' usage of Scripture, we find an impressive grasp of the richness that the biblical tradition has to offer a contemporary ecological hermeneutic. While there is a certain amount of proof-texting, as is a common approach to Scripture in Vatican documents, *Laudato Si'* attends faithfully to the context of the Biblical texts it utilises. As we read this document we have a genuine sense that Pope Francis has reflected deeply on the biblical tradition and has integrated it authentically with his urgent concern for the environment. True to his papal namesake, St Francis of Assisi, Pope Francis allows his delight in the wonders of God's creation, human and non-human, to shine through this document. And from that delight comes his concomitant belief that environmental responsibility is of the divine will, as attested in the biblical tradition.

The Call of *Laudato Si'* for Christian Witness to the Gospel: Expanding our Eschatological Mission to Sustainable Living with Earth

Abigail L Lofte

Introduction

In *Laudato Si'*, Pope Francis focuses on the doctrines of creation and eschatology as he implores Christians everywhere to care for creation through responsible action founded on wonder and awe of the universe. He appeals to the eternal, creative Word, risen and glorified, as the rationale for seeing God in all things and as the end toward which all are drawn. Pope Francis refers to eschatological hope as the driving force behind Christian witness in human relationships with Earth as we seek to create just and merciful relationships where we have failed in the past.

However, despite the overall power of *Laudato Si'*, Pope Francis' argument would gain a deeper potency had he more explicitly drawn on the resurrection of Christ. As it is, *Laudato Si'* invokes the idea of "resurrection" only once, in its discussion of the Eternal Sabbath.[1] In this article I explore the implications of Christ's resurrection for prompting Christian witness to ecological devastation as we strive to live the Good News with integrity. Below, I first draw on Edward Schillebeeckx's theology of resurrection and mission to understand the importance of the risen Lord for sending the disciples out to renew the world. Second, I turn to Thomas Berry's theological anthropology to understand how twenty-first century people must relate to

---

1. Francis, *Laudato Si'* (On Care for our Common Home), Vatican Website, 24 May 2015, para. 237. At <http://w2.vatican.va/content/francesco/en/encyclicals/documents/papa-francesco_20150524_enciclica-laudato-si.html>. Accessed 1 June 2016.

Earth to establish mutually enhancing relationships. Finally, I trace a missiology guided by eschatological hope and manifested in Christian witness, thereby expanding the disciples' mission to include our relationship with Earth so that we also seek a renewed, sustainable future with the planet, prioritising justice and mercy as we witness to the Gospel in our own time.

Edward Schillebeeckx on Resurrection and Mission

Edward Schillebeeckx's resurrection theology serves as a helpful expansion of Pope Francis' theology of missionary renewal, seen clearly in *Evangelii Gaudium*, and furthered through care for our common home in *Laudato Si'*. Proposing a vision that is forward-looking but still rooted in reality, the church on Earth becomes necessary for realizing our eschatological future in a collaborative way.[2] Schillebeeckx constructs his method by exploring the diversity of human experience and the varieties of socio-cultural and historical circumstances that shape human existence.[3] Christian belief must speak to negative contrast experiences of suffering and injustice in historical consciousness because seeking a better future is impossible without acknowledging the reality of suffering, a point echoed by Pope Francis.[4] The experience of suffering presupposes a desire for happiness, while the experience of injustice presupposes the capacity for integrity. As such, in an effort to overcome this suffering, humans must anticipate a meaningful future achieved through our own activity,

---

2. *Laudato Si'*, 3.
3. Roger D Haight, *The Future of Christology* (New York: Continuum, 2005), 108–109. Haight contends that Schillebeeckx's method affirms the diversity of embodied human experience, particularly that of suffering, which is more helpful for developing a resurrection theology offering hope for our times. On the other hand Rahner, who is heavily relied upon in eco-theology to re-imagine doctrinal commitments, employs a method hinging upon the self-transcending character of the human person through highly developed consciousness. Whereas Rahner assumes a universal human experience and a common way of participating in the nature of God, Schillebeeckx seeks a way of participation through lifestyles in consonance with the will of God that create more meaningful existence on Earth right now.
4. Mary Catherine Hilkert, 'The Threatened *Humanum* as *Imago Dei*: Anthropology and Christian Ethics', in *Edward Schillebeeckx and Contemporary Theology*, edited by Lieven Boeve, Frederiek Depoortere, Stephan van Erp (London: T&T Clark, 2010), 130–132; *Laudato Si'*, 13.

which simultaneously unlocks the way to this future, expecting humans to act more humanely and to work toward the elimination of the causes of injustice.[5] Schillebeeckx considers Jesus as the historical parable of God who, through his personal existence, conveys divine realities to others' personal experience, which culminates most fruitfully in the disciples' experience of Christ in the Easter appearances.

Schillebeeckx makes a helpful distinction between the Easter event and 'the Easter experience', noting that in the Easter experience Jesus is the agent who makes himself seen by the disciples and who is the centre and source of this experience of grace, perceived by them through the eyes of faith. 'Their Easter experience is an "enthusiastic" one of the Lord actively present in their community, and soon to come: a *maranatha* experience. They do not ponder the question whether Jesus has been brought from the realm of the dead by way of a resurrection, a "rapture" or (on the Greek model) by God. He is in any case "with God."'[6] The Easter experience of the disciples becomes the source for them of God's unfolding revelation and self-communication of grace, and it is this place of encounter that is the bedrock of their response back to God in faith.

Schillebeeckx, therefore, asserts that Jesus Christ is best understood in the context of the Christian community that began with the disciples and endures today. As a twofold event, the resurrection contains within it the historical dimension of assembling and forming a community of disciples and the spiritual dimension of commitment to renewal of the world through a lifestyle in co-operation with the Kingdom of God. Pope Francis also calls for renewal through common life, though without any explicit reference to the early church community, but as Schillebeeckx notes, the life of Jesus is fused with the life of the Church so that the living Lord in the resurrection, present through the Holy Spirit, enlivens and builds a community of believers in solidarity with people everywhere.[7]

---

5. Edward Schillebeeckx, 'Naar een "definitieve toekomst": belofte en menselijke bemiddeling"', in *Toekomst van de religie—Religie van de toekomst?* (Brussels: Desclée de Brouwer, 1972), 45–47, quoted in Robert J Schreiter, 'Contrast Experiences', in *The Schillebeeckx Reader*, edited and translated by Robert J Schreiter (New York: Crossroad, 1987), 54–56.

6. Edward Schillebeeckx, *Jesus: An Experiment in Christology*, translted by Hubert Hoskins (New York: Crossroad, 1981), 396.

7. Edward Schillebeeckx, *Church: The Human Story of God*, translated by John Bowden (New York: Crossroad, 1990), 155; *Laudato Si'*, 118.

As the Church today we remember the Paschal Mystery of Christ through the practice of becoming his disciples through participation in his mission by 'responding to one's own new situations from out of an intense experience of God'.[8] This moves beyond imitating Christ by doing *what* he did, to doing *as* he did by responding to the needs around us that arise in socio-historical contexts. The church embraces a living and active remembrance of the Paschal Mystery of Christ directed toward the future so that we, the community, become the living symbol and agent of Christ's ongoing action in the world.

Orthopraxis becomes the manifestation of God's saving love that we express through our practical, day-to-day living where we love as God loves, without distinction or division. As Jesus mediates God through his ministry to others, we are called to witness to the coming Kingdom of God through our care, based on the example of his life. Conversion, through discernment in prayer, to new beliefs and behaviours founded on faith in this future is required, a point echoed by Pope Francis who understands the need for an integrative approach, apart from simply technical solutions, to ensure a lasting change.[9] This leads to a lifestyle of the Kingdom where we work toward a renewal of the world through commitments to living in consonance with the life of Jesus, which includes preparadness to suffer in solidarity with, and on behalf of, others. By uniting ourselves in solidarity with those enduring oppression and struggling in structural poverty, the church is where it ought to be: at the fore of conflict giving witness to the power of the Gospel to save and transform.[10] Aligning ourselves with the will of God, we achieve meaningful lives and ultimate happiness by taking responsibility for the wellbeing of others, even though it requires sacrifice from us.

Thomas Berry and Theological Anthropology or Viable Human Life

Thomas Berry's work provides a helpful framework for the application of Schillebeeckx's work for the twenty-first century concerns

---

8.   Edward Schillebeeckx, *Christ: The Experience of Jesus as Lord*, translated by John Bowden (New York: Crossroad, 1983), 641–642.
9.   Schillebeeckx, *Jesus*, 154; *Laudato Si'*, 111.
10. Schillebeeckx, *Church*, 184.

regarding ecological degradation and climate change. Berry contributes a much more practical and informed voice to the conversation about the seriousness of the rift in the relationship between humans and the rest of creation, identified also by Pope Francis, and underscores the urgency of recovering a sense of a sacred universe to motivate our action.[11] Through our lifestyles, we have divided the world between the realm of the human and that of everything else, even though all creatures share the same Earth. Ongoing human existence is bound up with the life of everything else, therefore we must prioritise reconciliation, which requires a sense of beauty and wonder at this gracious world that sustains us physically, as well as spiritually, and is the revelation of God. Pope Francis, quoting the Australian bishops, believes that conversion, leading to reconciliation, will move humans toward this reunification.[12] Our great work now is to devise a new way of human life on Earth befitting the home of God among Us, seeking a way into the future that is mutually enhancing for our species and planet.[13]

Berry describes humanity as those creatures in whom the universe becomes self-reflective through a special consciousness and self-awareness, capable of understanding and expressing itself within the story of evolutionary development and formed in the context of a broad ecological community.[14] Humanity cannot exist and flourish in isolation; we require an ecological sociality in which to learn from others how to live well, about ourselves as a species, and, through

---

11. Thomas Berry, 'Christianity's Role in the Earth Project' in *Christianity and Ecology*, edited by Dieter T Hessel and Rosemary Radford Ruether (Cambridge: Harvard University Press, 2000),131, 134; *Laudato Si'*, 18, 84–88.

12. *Laudato Si'*, 218.

13. Denis Edwards is concerned that Berry's shift in focus from anthropocentrism to a more inclusive biocentric vision reduces the uniqueness of humans in the community of species. He suggests that Berry's vision would instead benefit from becoming more theocentric, allowing for a broader understanding of relationship. See Denis Edwards, *Partaking of God: Trinity, Evolution, and Ecology* (Collegeville: Liturgical Press, 2014), 167. Anne Marie Dalton, however, disagrees with Edwards' assessment and instead sees Berry's move as simply a call to conversion, requiring sacrifice from humans to realise this vision. See Anne Marie Dalton, *A Theology for the Earth: The Contributions of Thomas Berry and Bernard Lonergan* (Ottawa: University of Ottawa Press, 1999), 175–176.

14. Thomas Berry and Thomas Clarke, *Befriending Earth: A Theology of Reconciliation between Humans and the Earth*, edited by Stephen Dunn and Anne Lonergan (Mystic, CT: Twenty-Third Publications, 1991), 21.

reflection on this community, create meaning for our lives. While Pope Francis includes a social dimension in his ecological approach, the vision of *Laudato Si'* is restricted to only the natural world and the poor, not widening the scope beyond this locality to the entire cosmos.[15] Seeking this mutually enhancing future for humanity, and the rest of creation, requires a retrieval of our basic story of how this species came into existence in the context of the universe's becoming and how all creatures might together move forward.[16] Humanity must critically assess this situation, including priorities and values, and seek meaningful experiences and relationships with Earth's communion of subjects. Therefore, Berry suggests a reinvention of the human being at the species level as the starting point for revitalising human-Earth relationships.

Reinventing the human will require significant work as radical, life-affirming responses are implemented for healing the division between the larger world and us. 'The historical mission of our time', Berry asserts, 'is to reinvent the human—at the species level, with critical reflection, within the community of life-systems, in a time-developmental context, by means of story and shared dream experience.'[17] To reinvent the human affirms the versatility of the species for learning skills that can be taught, appropriated, and utilised for ongoing development. This, however, has become stifled by existing cultural norms making the planet subservient to humans. As such, a species-level reinvigoration is required of humans, more fundamental to us than any cultural achievement, to recover what is most innate to our species—gaining awareness of others and ourselves in the context of an ecological communion of subjects. Pope Francis agrees that a rebuilding of cultural identities is necessary for resituating the human within the wider planetary context.[18] Berry asserts that to begin this task, we humans must first decentralise ourselves and then reflect critically, through self-reflective consciousness, on the implications of this for relationships. The urgency of this task compels us to appreciate Earth's life systems as one community

---

15. *Laudato Si'*, 49.
16. Thomas Berry, *Dream of the Earth* (San Francisco: Sierra Club Books, 1988), 124.
17. Thomas Berry, *The Great Work: Our Way into the Future* (New York: Three Rivers Press, 1999), 159–165.
18. *Laudato Si'*, 105, 111–112, 114.

of differentiated beings, which includes humans, that share one future together. Taking into account our historical and cosmological context, the existence of every life form is bound up with that of all others and must affirm the uniqueness of individuals and communities, value the subjectivity of each being, and realise the necessity of relationship for the entire Earth community.

Shifting the focus to Earth-centered priorities, Berry identifies a number of ways in which human-Earth relationships might alter to include lifestyles in harmony with Earth's processes, forming a viable human existence on the planet and leading to the ecological culture that Pope Francis seeks.[19] The opposition of ecological groups advocating for Earth to industrial corporations seeking rights to resources, Berry and Pope Francis note, is the central issue of our time and that, because of their longevity and widespread activity, persuading corporations to make these necessary changes will be very difficult.[20] While Pope Francis identifies a number of areas that ought to be re-examined, Berry calls for a total overhaul of four fundamental areas that must change if there is any hope of preserving and enhancing life for the Earth community.[21] First, protecting natural resources from commodification by economic systems requires, fundamentally, that humans develop relationships with nature that persuade us, through beauty, to care for it through intense concern and vigorous action for addressing damage already inflicted. Second, shifting the focus of the legal system to advocate for the needs of Earth, outside of human rights to its possession, creates new conditions for the functioning and wellbeing of Earth that promotes just and mutually enhancing relationships for planetary life. Third, reimagining the educational system so that Earth becomes the primary teacher and sensitises students to the intimations of the planet becomes the new locus for forming humans to use learned knowledge and skills on behalf of the entire Earth community in all activities. Fourth, altering the purview of the medical profession to see human health intrinsically bound up with planetary health necessitates a method of treating patients co-operatively with Earth without overwhelming the body or the planet with toxic materials. If systems are reoriented toward the priority of flourishing planetary life, beyond the human,

---

19. *Laudato Si'*, 111.
20. Berry, *Great Work*, 59; *Laudato Si'*, 13–14.
21. Berry, *Great Work*, 60–69.

there may be a chance of enduring as a human species, viably, on Earth.

Implications for *Laudato Si'*

While Pope Francis rightly believes that faith convictions motivate care for Earth and the vulnerable by appealing to the Genesis stories, among others, I believe, as Schillebeeckx has shown, that the strength of the Christian story for compelling us to act lies also in the resurrection accounts and the Easter experience of the disciples.[22] As a story that educates, heals, guides, and disciplines, the resurrection narrative affirms the miraculous character of Jesus' ministry, confirms the authority by which he was sent, and invites all who believe into participation with this mystery anticipating its fullness on the Last Day. The resurrection, begun in Christ, and ongoing in the life of the church is what gives the Christian person identity and provides the model and expectation for how we ought to be in the world to further this mission, as a sign of God's continuous activity and a symbol of the life we expect in the General Resurrection. The resurrected Christ is the prism through which we must understand the contours of our proleptic future.

Pope Francis identifies a number of arenas in the vision he lays out, which require change including environmental and international communities, national and local policies, decision-making, politics and economics, and the relationship between science and religion.[23] He proposes these be addressed by cultivating a new lifestyle through education, ecological conversion, reassessing standards for quality of life, harmonious relationships, and the sacramental life of the church.[24] Berry, however, in his reinvention contributes a more fundamental reimagination of language used to express values and priorities, extending to those of Earth.[25] Industrial corporations have co-opted language to creatively advertise the glories of the modernised world while also being deceptively positive about ecological realities. Progress, for example, indicates sophisticated scientific understandings of the universe, increased interpersonal development

---

22. *Laudato Si'*, 64.
23. *Laudato Si'*, chapter 5.
24. *Laudato Si'*, chapter 6.
25. Berry, *Great Work*, 62–63.

through social media, and access to more comprehensive health care and longer life expectancies. Through technology we can produce more, and faster. We can travel greater distances in a shorter period of time with relative comfort. We continue to progress as though this is virtuous and with the belief that, because it is within human capability, it is justified. Pope Francis points out that the right use of power and responsibility is key for living the Christian mission in relationship, but Berry adds a jarring point that progress has occurred at the cost of stripping away the resources of the natural world and led to an 'Earth-deficit'.[26] In the quest to make what Berry calls, "wonderworld," through unlimited human achievement, "waste-world" has been created where human progress seems to *only* function at the desolation of the planet.[27] Therefore, a reimagining of values, and how they are communicated, is necessary for enacting this missiological vision put forth by Pope Francis.

Pope Francis notes that, imitating the sacrifice of Jesus, our faith motivates harmonious and sacrificial living and that, for human-Earth relationships, consumption must be replaced with sacrifice.[28] Schillebeeckx's vision contributes a dimension of sacrificial suffering, noting that a hallmark of discipleship in the early Christian community was a spiritual sacrifice of suffering in solidarity with others, Christians having committed themselves to a worthy cause, that is, a mission founded on the life of Jesus of Nazareth.[29] As the church today furthering the mission of the disciples, Christians are called to a vocation of obedience to the one who beckons us to participation, and through suffering we live the implications of and responsibilities for this cause. Living out of the resurrection vision furthered in the disciples' ministry, coupled with rethinking human-Earth relationships by reimagining existing structures, enhances the vision put forth by Pope Francis in *Laudato Si'* by offering a more continuous thread from our Christian confession of resurrection to the embodiment of this in daily living with the Earth community.

In doing so, the urgency of climate change inspires more than attitudes of generosity and reflection that lead to minimal action, relying instead on hope for God's inclusion of plants and animals, with hu-

---

26. Berry, *Dream of the Earth*, 72; *Laudato Si'*, 68–69.
27. Berry, *Great Work*, 68.
28. *Laudato Si'*, 9, 201, 220.
29. Schillebeeckx, *Christ*, 227.

manity's transformation, in the *eschaton*. Without significant action, the promotion of relationships between humans and Earth founded on love, respect, and care in hope of a final future founded upon the instantiation of this in the resurrection of Jesus carries no actual religious or political consequences. Failing to take the conversation about orthopraxis beyond a list of virtues allows the resurrection to become a nice story we tell ourselves to feel good about the future without prompting any lifestyle changes. This has the potential to become counterproductive as it lulls us into a false sense of complacency about the future where, because we believe that God will work everything out in the end, we really do not have to do much to claim that we are doing our part. However, NT Wright asserts, the 'Gospels do not say Jesus is raised, therefore we're going to heaven or therefore we're going to be raised. They say Jesus is raised, therefore God's new creation has begun and we've got a job to do.'[30] Without taking into consideration real religious and political consequences for living resurrection faith, the Christian eschatological vision remains anaemic and we become trapped in the cycle of promoting love, solidarity, and respect without having to do anything about it. What I suspect we really want for relationships with Earth is justice, certainly, but committing to justice necessitates committing to the hard work of living differently and prioritising something other than immediate human desires—a demanding lifestyle, indeed, for the developed world.

Conclusion

This lifestyle of the reinvented, viable human that promotes restoring integrity in relationships and guiding reality to a retrieval of values that protects humans, and the whole community of species, for healthy existence in the future is a way to live the orthopraxis that Pope Francis is seeking. As a community of believers oriented toward the way of Jesus Christ, Christians are tasked with seeking a better, renewed future through participation in his life and ministry. In an ecological context Berry identifies how the lifestyle of the King-

---

30. NT Wright and John Dominic Crossan, 'The Resurrection: Historical Event or Theological Explanation? A Dialogue', in *The Resurrection of Jesus: John Dominic Crossan and NT Wright in Dialogue*, edited by Robert B Steward (Minneapolis: Fortress Press, 2006), 21.

dom can be personified through a re-evaluation of priorities, rights, roles, and responsibilities to the entire planet and offers a framework through which to interpret them. Schillebeeckx's theology of the Easter experience and its significance for Christian life, with its application to the areas identified by Berry, ultimately creates a much stronger theology for *Laudato Si'* that allows for the significance of the resurrection. Moving beyond attitudinal shifts of love, care, and respect for creation that will know fullness in the Eternal Sabbath, Pope Francis with Schillebeeckx and Berry require dynamic activity, fuelled by strongly held beliefs, based on a lifestyle committed to co-operation with God.

Bibliography

Berry, Thomas and Thomas Clarke. *Befriending Earth: A Theology of Reconciliation between Humans and the Earth.* Edited by Stephen Dunn and Anne Lonergan (Mystic, CT: Twenty-Third Publications, 1991

Berry, Thomas. 'Christianity's Role in the Earth Project'. In *Christianity and Ecology.* Edited by Dieter T Hessel and Rosemary Radford Ruether (Cambridge: Harvard University Press, 2000), 127–134.

_____. *Dream of the Earth.* (San Francisco: Sierra Club Books, 1988).

_____. *The Great Work: Our Way into the Future.* (New York: Three Rivers Press, 1999).

Dalton, Anne Marie. *A Theology for the Earth: The Contributions of Thomas Berry and Bernard Lonergan.* (Ottawa: University of Ottawa Press, 1999).

Edwards, Denis. *Partaking of God: Trinity, Evolution, and Ecology.* (Collegeville: Liturgical Press, 2014).

Haight, Roger D. *The Future of Christology.* (New York: Continuum, 2005).

Hilkert, Mary Catherine. 'The Threatened *Humanum* as *Imago Dei*: Anthropology and Christian Ethics'. In *Edward Schillebeeckx and Contemporary Theology.* Edited by Lieven Boeve, Frederiek Depoortere, Stephan van Erp. (London: T&T Clark, 2010), 127–141.

Pope Francis. *Laudato Si'* (On Care for our Common Home). Vatican Website. 24 May 2015. <http://w2.vatican.va/content/francesco/en/encyclicals/documents/papa-francesco_20150524_enciclica-laudato-si.html>. Accessed 1 June 2016.

Schillebeeckx, Edward. *Christ: The Experience of Jesus as Lord.* Translated by John Bowden. (New York: Crossroad, 1983).

_____. *Church: The Human Story of God.* Translated by John Bowden. (New York: Crossroad, 1990).

_____. *Jesus: An Experiment in Christology.* Translated by Hubert Hoskins. (New York: Crossroad, 1981).

_____. 'Naar een "definitieve toekomst": belofte en menselijke bemiddeling'. In *Toekomst van de religie—Religie van de toekomst?*, 37-55. (Brussels: Desclée de Brouwer, 1972).

Schreiter, Robert J. 'Contrast Experiences'. In *The Schillebeeckx Reader.* Edited and translated by Robert J Schreiter. (New York: Crossroad, 1987), 54–56.

Wright, NT and John Dominic Crossan. 'The Resurrection: Historical Event or Theological Explanation? A Dialogue'. In *The Resurrection of Jesus: John Dominic Crossan and NT Wright in Dialogue.* Edited by Robert B Steward. (Minneapolis: Fortress Press, 2006), 16–47.

Anticipating the Renewal of Earth: Theology and Science in *Laudato Si'*

Ted Peters

Introduction

The 24 May 2015 Encyclical Letter of Pope Francis, *Laudato Si'*, is a triumph of biblical interpretation, theological discernment, ethical analysis, interdisciplinary scholarship, spiritual direction, and passionate zeal. The pope calls all peoples on the planet to repentance from shortsighted and selfish practices that are destroying Earth's capacity to support life. He also calls for conversion to an eco-ethic that will lead to a cultural revolution and renewal of our terrestrial home. In this commentary and analysis, the role of natural science in the encyclical's theological structure and ethical argument will be analyzed and supplemented. Pope Francis follows the model of repentance and conversion familiar to classical Christianity and duplicates it for the peoples of the world, for both Christians and all others. He calls for a single global community of moral deliberation in which the Church will offer one, but not the only, voice.

Papal encyclicals deserve close reading. Especially this one. The situation is grave. Sister Earth is suffering from a mortal disease. That disease is the human race. The need for a life-saving cure is urgent. In *Laudato Si'*, Pope Francis is driving the ambulance to the scene.

Laudato Si' is lengthy, complex, nuanced, and powerful. It includes scriptural exegesis, Moral Theology, and Christian Spirituality right along with natural science, politics, economics, and cultural analysis. Only an erudite and compassionate individual or team of intellectuals would be capable of composing such a landmark document. I, for one, am grateful that the Holy See has mediated this prophetic gift to our contemporary world.

In what follows we will look briefly at two salient themes in *Laudato Si'*, its theology of repentance and its employment of natural science.[1] Science plays two roles in the Pontiff's letter. On the one hand, the Pontiff fears the hegemony of scientism. Like a speeding train without an engineer, our scientised and technologised civilisation is cannon balling toward ecological self-destruction. The pope does not wave a stop flag. Rather, quite prophetically, the pope admonishes us to put extra-scientific moral values and human compassion into the engineer's seat and directs us to another track. On the other hand, the Pontiff so mixes environmental science and social ethics that they work cooperatively in a seamless unity. He demonstrates by example the dynamics of partnership between science and moral resolve.

The doctrine of creation plays a large role in *Laudato Si'*, while eschatology plays a minimal role. Might the encyclical letter be enhanced by additional treatment of God's promise of a new creation?

Vatican Theology in *Laudato Si'*

The Holy Father feels a sense of urgency. What is the problem that urgently needs a remedy? The problem is sin. With allusions to St Francis of Assisi, the Holy Father describes human sin as our failure to take care of our sister, Sister Earth. The ecological crisis of our planet is anthropogenic, caused by human arrogance and neglect.

> This sister now cries out to us because of the harm we have inflicted on her by our irresponsible use and abuse of the goods with which God has endowed her. We have come to see ourselves as her lords and masters, entitled to plunder her at will. The violence present in our hearts, wounded by sin, is also reflected in the symptoms of sickness evident in the soil, in the water, in the air and in all forms of life. This is why the earth herself, burdened and laid waste, is among the most abandoned and maltreated of our poor; she 'groans in travail' (Rom 8:22) (2).

What is the remedy for this expression of sin? The remedy begins with repentance and leads to conversion. By repenting, the human

---

1.   All citations are drawn from Pope Francis, *Laudato Si'* (24 May 2015) at http://w2.vatican.va/content/dam/francesco/pdf/encyclicals/documents/papa-francesco_20150524_enciclica-laudato-si_en.pdf (accessed19 December 2015).

race opens itself to the realization that all terrestrial life belongs to Planet Earth like a family belongs to its home. Earth is our home. Everyone one of us lives together in this common home, so we need a conversation or dialogue or planning session that involves every member of our planetary family.

> The urgent challenge to protect our common home includes a concern to bring the whole human family together to seek a sustainable and integral development, for we know that things can change.
> Humanity still has the ability to work together in building our common home.
> I urgently appeal, then, for a new dialogue about how we are shaping the future of our planet. We need a conversation which includes everyone, since the environmental challenge we are undergoing, and its human roots, concern and affect us all (13–14).

The papal call is for planetary conversation, dialogue, planning. Francis is serious. The Roman Catholic Church will not play a trump card, not demand its own way. Rather, the Church in cooperation with others will plan conjointly.

> There are certain environmental issues where it is not easy to achieve a broad consensus. Here I would state once more that the Church does not presume to settle scientific questions or to replace politics. But I am concerned to encourage an honest and open debate so that particular interests or ideologies will not prejudice the common good (188).

Honest debate. That's what the pope asks for. Are there preconditions? Yes, one. The precondition is conversion. This planetary dialogue should involve all those who have already become converted. Converted to what? Converted to justice for the poor and compassion for Sister Earth.

> This conversion calls for a number of attitudes which together foster a spirit of generous care, full of tenderness. First, it entails gratitude and gratuitousness, a recognition that the world is God's loving gift, and that we are called quietly to imitate his generosity in self-sacrifice and good works . . It also entails a loving awareness that we are not disconnected from the rest of creatures, but joined in a splendid universal communion . . . By developing our individual, God-given capacities, an ecological conversion can inspire us to greater cre-

ativity and enthusiasm in resolving the world's problems and in offering ourselves to God 'as a living sacrifice, holy and acceptable'
(Rom 12:1) (220).

Theologically speaking, in *Laudato Si'* Pope Francis takes the classical model of repentance from sin plus conversion to faith in Jesus
Christ and applies it to the ecological crisis. *Sin,* in this case, refers to
anthropogenic contributions to climate change and environmental
degradation. *Conversion,* in this case, refers to a new moral resolve
on the part of all peoples to care for the Earth and pursue justice for
the poor. The Pontiff is not responding to repentance with forgive-
ness, grace, or absolution. Rather, he is responding with a reiteration
of what the Scriptures call *law,* namely, the moral demand. In this
case the moral demand is to love Earth and the poor.

The pope's underlying anthropology is certainly not that of Refor-
mation Calvinists who begin with total depravity. Rather, the pope
holds that the human person is innately drawn toward the good, capable of doing the good. Moral persuasion seeks to fan the flames of
an inner spark of goodness.

> Human beings, while capable of the worst, are also capable of rising
> above themselves, choosing again what is good, and making a new
> start, despite their mental and social conditioning. We are able to take
> an honest look at ourselves, to acknowledge our deep dissatisfaction,
> and to embark on new paths to authentic freedom. No system can
> completely suppress our openness to what is good, true and beautiful,
> or our God-given ability to respond to his grace at work deep in our
> hearts (205).

No regeneration is required in the papal anthropology at work here.
The natural human being, according to *Laudato Si'*, is capable of rising to the challenge posed to us by the ecological crisis. The Pontiff is
employing moral persuasion to draw out the innate goodness in the
human soul and enlisting it in the service of repentance and conversion. The future of our planet may rest on the validity of this anthro-
pological assumption.

Science and Theology in *Laudato Si'*

What should be the relationship between science and theology, according to Pope Francis? He relies on what Ian G. Barbour calls the

dialogue model.[2] The Holy Father writes, 'Science and religion, with their distinctive approaches to understanding reality, can enter into an intense dialogue fruitful for both' (62). Underlying such a statement is a presupposition, which I dub the *two-language theory*. According to the two-language theory, we respect 'the sovereign territory of both science and theology' before engaging in a dialogue that could be fruitful for both.[3] When the Holy Father speaks of 'distinctive approaches to understanding reality', he presupposes that science and theology each speak a different language, so to speak. And each language should be respected for what it says. Once this respect is established, then authentic dialogue can begin.

The weakness with the two-language theory is that it may prevent acknowledging something very important, namely, science studies the same world that God is creating. There is but one reality, finally. And we need to press beyond the 'distinctive approaches' in order to ask reality itself to correct those approaches. This has led some scholars in the field of Theology and Science to propose going beyond dialogue to *creative mutual interaction* (CMI).[4] In sum, the papal model respects science and theology as distinctive approaches to our one reality, but it stops short of advocating creative mutual interaction.

The pope wants to sequester science within its own language. Why? Because he wants to preserve the independent integrity of theology's language. If science and science alone provides the narrative within which culture understands itself, then we will have no transcendental resources or moral resources to enlist in planetary renewal. Our culture must speak the language of faith and the language of human compassion if it is to regain the moral resolve necessary for planetary renewal.

Let me explain further. One of the cultural threats we confront today is scientism. Science turns into scientism when it claims more than it ought to claim. 'Scientism is fundamentally the transformation of the methodology of empirical science into a metaphysics, a move from the quantitative investigation of nature to the assumption that being is always quantitative. While the former is a legit-

---

2. Ian G Barbour, *Religion and Science: Historical and Contemporary Issues* (New York: Harper, 1997), 90–98.
3. Ted Peters, *Science, Theology, and Ethics* (Aldershot UK: Ashgate, 2003) 18.
4. Robert John Russell, *Cosmology from Alpha to Omega* (Minneapolis MN: Fortress Press, 2008), 22–23.

imate methodology, the latter is mere ideology', writes Dominican theologian Michael Dodds.[5] World Religions scholar, Huston Smith, weighs in. 'The problem is not science, but scientism—namely, to assume that what science turns up and can turn up is the sum of all there is'.[6] Although he does not specifically use the term, *scientism*, on the mind of Pope Francis is the risk that science might overreach.

> It cannot be maintained that empirical science provides a complete explanation of life, the interplay of all creatures and the whole of reality. This would be to breach the limits imposed by its own methodology (199).

Francis fears scientism not just among scientists but, even more so, as a cultural worldview. It has been too easy for our culture to sell its soul to the relentless march of science and technology under the banner of progress. Progress is soulless. Our culture must retrieve spiritual depth for progress to regain its proper value-led direction.

> All of this shows the urgent need for us to move forward in a bold cultural revolution. Science and technology are not neutral; from the beginning to the end of a process, various intentions and possibilities are in play and can take on distinct shapes. Nobody is suggesting a return to the Stone Age, but we do need to slow down and look at reality in a different way, to appropriate the positive and sustainable progress which has been made, but also to recover the values and the great goals swept away by our unrestrained delusions of grandeur (114).

This is a healthy caution, in my judgment. Christian theologians and ethicists must work hand-in-glove with today's best science, but they must keep their guard up against the hegemony of scientism. Genuine dialogue between authentic science and our best theology helps maintain both cooperation and caution. With less force, Pope Francis reiterates the position taken by his predecessor, Pope John Paul II: 'Scientism is the philosophical notion which refuses to admit

---

5. Michael J Dodds OP, *Unlocking Divine Action: Contemporary Science and Thomas Aquinas* (Washington DC: Catholic University Press of America, 2012), 51, n27.
6. Huston Smith, *The Way Things Are: Conversations with Huston Smith on the Spiritual Life,* edited by Phil Cousineau (Berkeley: University of California Press, 2003), 118.

the validity of forms of knowledge other than those of the positive sciences; and it relegates religious, theological, ethical, and aesthetic knowledge to the realm of mere fantasy.[7] In sum, embrace science but shun scientism.

Science and Ethics in *Laudato Si'*

Eco-ethicist Cynthia Moe-Lobeda alerts us: 'The moral crisis screams...*Homo sapiens* are using and degrading the planet's natural goods at a rate that Earth's ecosystems cannot sustain. We have generated an unsustainable relationship with our planetary home.'[8] Pope Francis has heard the scream. He wants to save our home.

In order to save our planetary home, Francis enlists both science and ethics.[9] Like a cookie baker mixing flour with sugar, the pontiff mixes science and ethics so naturally that together they produce a single taste. The science of climate change becomes the batter in his recipe. Into the science Francis stirs one of the most fitting concepts in Roman Catholic Moral Theology, the *Common Good*.

> The climate is a common good, belonging to all and meant for all. At the global level, it is a complex system linked to many of the essential conditions for human life. A very solid scientific consensus indicates that we are presently witnessing a disturbing warming of the climatic system. Humanity is called to recognize the need for changes of lifestyle, production and consumption, in order to combat this warming or at least the human causes which produce or aggravate it (23).

What do we mean by the *common good*? Pope Francis reminds us of the Second Vatican Council's attention to the *common good*.

An integral ecology is inseparable from the notion of the common good, a central and unifying principle of social ethics. The common

---

7.   Pope John Paul II, *Fides et Ratio*, at http://web.archive.org/web/20131001225220/http://www.vatican.va/edocs/ESL0036/_INDEX.HTM
8.   Cynthia D. Moe-Lobeda, *Resisting Structural Evil: Love as Ecological-Economic Vocation* (Minneapolis: Fortress, 2013) 31.
9.   Appeal to science is required by ethics. "The root problem is one of values, which implies that value-based religious institutions ought to have a part in the discussion," writes Carolyn King. But, unfortunately, so far the churches "offer scant leadership, because they are too often scientifically uninformed and distracted by internal issues." Carolyn M. King, *Habitat of Grace: Biology, Christianity and the Global Environmental Crisis* (Adelaide: ATF, 2002) 183.

good is 'the sum of those conditions of social life which allow social groups and their individual members relatively thorough and ready access to their own fulfillment'[10] The common good calls for social peace, the stability and security provided by a certain order which cannot be achieved without particular concern for distributive justice; whenever this is violated, violence always ensues. Society as a whole, and the state in particular, are [sic] obliged to defend and promote the common good (156–157).

With his term, *integral ecology,* the Pontiff integrates science with ethics along with integrating all relevant secular disciplines: the sciences, politics, economics, and social theory. All spaces on our planet belong to the moral sphere of the common good, and analysing what is at stake takes in all the academic disciplines. In addition to space, the common good also stretches out over time. 'The notion of the common good also extends to future generations' (159). The common good is as inclusive an ethical concept as one can conceive.

The pope rightly acknowledges the urgent need to establish a single global community of moral deliberation. Climate change and related ecological concerns are all global and intergenerational in scope, and only an inclusive community dedicated to the common good can lead our way forward. 'Climate change involves a complex global set of both causal practices and felt impacts', write John Dryzek, Richard Norgaard, and David Schlosberg, speaking for scientists and economists. 'And as such requires coherent global action–or, at a minimum, coordination across some critical mass of global players.'[11]

Added to the concept of the common good is the principle of subsidiarity. Persons at every level of our global society must bear their fitting responsibility for the common good, to be sure, but those with greater power and influence must assume greater responsibility and initiative. According to Francis, 'the principle of subsidiarity . . . grants freedom to develop the capabilities present at every level of society, while also demanding a greater sense of responsibility for the common good from those who wield greater power' (196).

Almost as if the Vatican and the Club of Rome are speaking in concert about integral ecology, *Laudato Si'* lists the elements in the

---

10. *Gaudium et Spes*, 26.
11. John S Dryzek, Richard B Norgaard, and David Schlosberg, eds., *The Oxford Handbook of Climate Change and Society* (Oxford UK: Oxford University Press, 2011), 12.

composite problem we have known since 1972 as the *world prob-lematique*:[12] diminishing fresh water supply; depletion of fishing re-serves as well as non-renewable energy sources; loss of biodiversity; urban pollution; rural pollution; unbridled economic growth; the globalized technological imperative; international debt; social disso-lution accompanied by loss of dignity, and the interaction between environmental degradation and degradation of the poor. Because we human beings are so embedded in nature, all disciplines which study nature become ethically relevant.

> When we speak of the "environment", what we really mean is a re-lationship existing between nature and the society which lives in it. Nature cannot be regarded as something separate from ourselves or as a mere setting in which we live. We are part of nature, included in it and thus in constant interaction with it. Recognizing the reasons why a given area is polluted requires a study of the workings of society, its economy, its behaviour patterns, and the ways it grasps reality. Given the scale of change, it is no longer possible to find a specific, discrete answer for each part of the problem. It is essential to seek comprehen-sive solutions which consider the interactions within natural systems themselves and with social systems (139).

With a seamless sweep of eloquence the Pontiff rallies support for scientific research right along with love for the creatures who live with us on the planet.

> Greater investment needs to be made in research aimed at under-standing more fully the functioning of ecosystems and adequately analyzing the different variables associated with any significant modi-fication of the environment. Because all creatures are connected, each must be cherished with love and respect, for all of us as living crea-tures are dependent on one another (42).

The Controversy over Population Growth

Many critics want to blame Roman Catholic family planning pol-icies for population overgrowth. If only Catholics would prac-tise birth control and abortion, then we could rid our planet of

---

12. Donella H Meadows *et al*, *The Limits to Growth* (New York: Universe Books, 1972); see: http://www.clubofrome.org/. See Ted Peters, *Futures: Human and Di-vine* (Louisville: Westminster John Knox Press, 1978).

the starving poor! But, Pope Francis will not let this criticism go by unanswered. Earth does not have a problem of food supply, he says. Rather, it has a problem of food distribution. The rich over-consume and over-pollute, leaving the stomachs of the poor empty.

> To blame population growth instead of extreme and selective consumerism on the part of some, is one way of refusing to face the issues. It is an attempt to legitimize the present model of distribution, where a minority believes that it has the right to consume in a way which can never be universalized, since the planet could not even contain the waste products of such consumption (50).

The food problem is not a population problem, says the pope; it is a justice problem. Our commitment to justice is a commitment to the poor and to the environment alike.

Attention to the science supports the Pontiff's position. It is widely assumed that global population is growing exponentially and this is leading to starvation. But, some scientists call this a *myth*. 'The human population has not and is not growing exponentially and is unlikely to do so', we read in the journal, *Nature*. 'The world's population is now growing at just half the rate it was before 1965 . . . The world's population also has enough to eat.' That is to say, despite the widespread belief that exponential population growth exceeds the planet's capacity to feed us, the data indicates otherwise. What is actually at stake is a 'question about poverty'.[13] In short, the Pontiff has his facts straight. The planet today produces enough food for everyone to enjoy nourishment. This means that starvation is, at bottom, a justice issue.

Our commitment to justice extends also to the unborn. The Holy Father asks rhetorically, 'How can we genuinely teach the importance of concern for other vulnerable beings, however troublesome or inconvenient they may be, if we fail to protect a human embryo, even when its presence is uncomfortable and creates difficulties?' 120) We must protect the planet, the poor, and the unborn.

---

13. Megan Scudellari, 'Myths that will not die', in *Nature*, 528:7582 (17 December 2015): 322–325 (325).

Spirituality and Ethics in *Laudato Si'*

Science is not the only partner for ecological ethics. So also is spirituality. In fact, without spirituality, conversion to planetary consciousness and moral zeal will flag.

In order for spring flowers to blossom on a cherry tree, the tree must be rooted in fertile soil. So also, ethics must be rooted in spirituality. The common good is rooted in gratitude for God's gracious gift of a planet blossoming with life and beauty and energy. God-consciousness fertilises moral consciousness. Without God consciousness and its accompanying gratitude, we humans woull follow after false gods, actually gods of our own manufacture. Spiritual sensitivity is aware that God is present objectively, in the world.

> A spirituality which forgets God as all-powerful and Creator is not acceptable. That is how we end up worshipping earthly powers, or ourselves usurping the place of God, even to the point of claiming an unlimited right to trample his creation underfoot. The best way to restore men and women to their rightful place, putting an end to their claim to absolute dominion over the earth, is to speak once more of the figure of a Father who creates and who alone owns the world. Otherwise, human beings will always try to impose their own laws and interests on reality (75).

In addition, spiritual sensitivity is aware that God is present subjectively, in the intimacy of our own soul.

> God is intimately present to each being, without impinging on the autonomy of his creature, and this gives rise to the rightful autonomy of earthly affairs (80).

Eschatology and Ethics

Eschatology plays a negligible role in *Laudato Si'*. But it is not absent. Note how the Pontiff anticipates a fulfilment to be brought about by God, and then he leverages this against today's human hubris. Because the ultimate future of our world is in God's hands, it would be a mistake for the present generation of humans to think that we and we alone are responsible.

> The ultimate destiny of the universe is in the fullness of God, which has already been attained by the risen Christ, the measure of the maturity

of all things. Here we can add yet another argument for rejecting every tyrannical and irresponsible domination of human beings over other creatures. The ultimate purpose of other creatures is not to be found in us. Rather, all creatures are moving forward with us and through us towards a common point of arrival, which is God, in that transcendent fullness where the risen Christ embraces and illumines all things. Human beings, endowed with intelligence and love, and drawn by the fullness of Christ, are called to lead all creatures back to their Creator (83).

When it comes to eschatology, Francis places our cosmic and planetary future into God's hands, where it belongs. However, this stands in counterpoint to the central thrust of *Laudato Si'*, which focuses on the innate human capacity for doing what is good for the planet. The papal invitation is for a non-eschatological self-renewal and planetary renewal. Eschatology, in contrast, consists of a promise of divine, not human-achieved, transformation. Eschatological fulfillment and environmental renewal are not the same thing, to be sure; but, we may ask: are they are connected?

Perhaps a couple paragraphs about eschatology and its importance to creation are in order. Theologically, God's promise of a future completion of the creation influences the course of creation's history in the past and present. Or, to say it in reverse, the eschatological consummation of all things provides the end—end as completion and as goal—of the ongoing story of God's creative work. The past, present, and future of Earth gains its definition and value from its place in the future fulfilment of the whole of reality. Whether the members of *Homo sapiens* are successful at saving their current home or not, the full redemption of Earth's history will come as a future gift of God.

God's work as creator will not be finished until the creation attains its full definition in the eschatological fulfilment. We on Earth today are still on the way to experiencing the fullness of creation, a creation which will be completed only when God's creative work is completed. When the cosmos is redeemed, it will be created.

By *creation* we refer to the cosmos, not to planet Earth in isolation. The Earth is but a pale blue dot, to borrow Carl Sagan's imagery, within an unfathomably huge cosmic collection of star systems, galaxies, clusters of galaxies and beyond.[14] Indicated in the New Tes-

---

14. Carl Sagan, *Pale Blue Dot: A Vision of the Human Future in Space* (New York: Random House, 1994), 8.

tament by 'kingdom of God' or 'new creation', this final future has been proleptically anticipated by Jesus' Easter resurrection. New Testament historian NT Wright makes this clear. 'The central Christian affirmation is that what the creator God has done in Jesus Christ, and supremely in his resurrection, is what he intends to do for the whole world—meaning, by "world", the entire cosmos with all its history.'[15] An eco-ethic is geocentric, whereas eschatology is cosmocentric.

The Christian theologian interprets all of creation through the Cross and Resurrection. Creation will not be what God intends it to be until the new creation finishes the redeeming work already begun in the Easter resurrection. Denis Edwards makes this clear. 'The resurrection, and the final participation of creation in it, had always been the very meaning of creation. The resurrection is that for which the processes and regularities of the natural world exist. The God of resurrection is the God of creation.'[16] In sum, the eschatological future of the cosmos will complete God's creative work as promised to us in the Easter resurrection of Jesus. What happened to Jesus in becoming raised from the dead is a prolepsis of what will happen to nature and history at the advent of the new creation. To view the resurrected Jesus is to view the world's future.

The Holy Father rightly relies upon this futuristic ontology when he says, 'The ultimate destiny of the universe is in the fullness of God, which has already been attained by the risen Christ, the measure of the maturity of all things' (83). But, curiously, this anticipation of a future that measures up to Christ plays no substantive role in the pope's ecological ethics. Could it?

I believe it could. What the eschatological vision adds to the concept of the common good is grounding in the divine promise. The good will last. The good will win. Pursuing the good today ties us ontologically to what is everlasting. Aggressively pursuing the renewal of Earth's capacity to support life invisibly draws energy from God's gracious gift of life and new life. The tranformative power of God's future is available to us now should we wish to invoke it.

---

15. NT Wright, "Cosmic Future: Progress or Despair? *From Resurrection to Return: Perspectives from Theology and Science on Christian Eschatology,* edited by James Haire, Christine Ledger, and Stephen Picard (Adelaide: ATF Press, 2007), 5–31 (16-17).

16. Denis Edwards, *How God Acts: Creation, Redemption, and Special Divine Action* (Minneapolis: Fortress Press, 2010), 104.

Failure on the part of the human race today will not abort the eschatological establishment of the common good promised us in the Easter resurrection. In short, the establishing of the common good belongs to our future as a gift of redemptive grace. For the present generation to embrace the common good in the face of anthropogenic sin is to embrace destiny, truth, and final reality.

Conclusion

The Encyclical Letter of Pope Francis, *Laudato Si'*, is a triumph of ethical passion buttressed by biblical interpretation, theological construction, multi-disciplinary investigation, and spiritual discernment. According to our theological analysis, we have seen how the Holy Father has translated the classical model of repentance and conversion into a prophetic call for all peoples on the planet to repent of short-sighted and selfish practices that are destroying Earth's capacity to support life. He further calls for conversion to an eco-ethic that will lead to a cultural revolution and renewal of our terrestrial home. According to our scientific analysis, we have seen that the Holy Father cautions us against embracing scientism and the idolatry of directionless progress. Further, he presses the best science into the service of an ethics of care for the Earth and care for the poor.

Our analysis should not consort with paralysis. *Laudato Si'* is a call to arms, a rally for action. Nearly four decades ago secular prophets—such as the members of the Club of Rome—rose up to urge the world to repent of its consumptive sins and convert to a sustainable global economy. The world did not listen. Those prophecies of doom are today closer to their fulfilment. Now, it's the Bishop of Rome donning the mantle of the prophet and repeating the same prophetic warnings. During the period in which the world has refused to listen the *world problematique* has only worsened. Our earthly home is in urgent need of care and repair. That's the unmistakable message of *Laudato Si'*.

Reflections on *Laudato Si'*

Frank Brennan

Pope Francis's first, and to date only, encyclical *Laudato Si'* is on the topic 'care for our common home'. The Murdoch press was quick to label it a 'Papal prescription for a flawed economic order' with the subtitle of *The Weekend Australian* editorial declaring, 'The church should not belong to the green-left fringe'.[1]

I will address three questions about the encyclical which contains more than its fair share of internal contradictions. I commence with the observation by Francis:

> In those countries which should be making the greatest changes in consumer habits, young people have a new ecological sensitivity and a generous spirit, and some of them are making admirable efforts to protect the environment. At the same time, they have grown up in a milieu of extreme consumerism and affluence which makes it difficult to develop other habits. We are faced with an educational challenge.[2]

We are all on a learning curve here. Francis is challenging us to be better educated and informed, but also to take practical action individually and collectively.

Why Would Pope Francis Write to Everyone?

Pope Francis is not the first pope to address a social encyclical to everyone. Pope John Paul II addressed his 1988 encyclical *Sollicitudo Rei Socialis* to members of the Church and to 'all people of good will'. Pope Benedict XVI did the same with his 2009 encyclical *Caritas in Veritate*. In comparison with his predecessors however, Francis has been more inclusive in the process of writing the encyclical and in the

---

1. Editorial, *The Weekend Australian*, 27–28 June 2015.
2. Pope Francis, *Laudato Si'*, 209.

final content of the document. He quotes from seventeen different conferences of Catholic bishops. This was rarely done by his predecessors. He is at pains to indicate that he is collaborative and that he takes the principle of subsidiarity very seriously. He convened meetings of various types of experts, including scientists, economists and political scientists. He is not afraid to indicate that the final product is something of a committee job, with various authors. He notes, 'Although each chapter will have its own subject and specific approach, it will also take up and re-examine important questions previously dealt with . . . [Q]uestions will not be dealt with once and for all, but reframed and enriched again and again.' [3] Being the final redactor of the text, he has felt free to interpolate some very folksy advice from time to time—from the need to use less air conditioning, to the appropriateness of consumer boycotts on certain products, to the desirability of saying grace before and after meals. He has also taken the liberty of inserting some very blunt, evocative images of environmental and economic devastation: 'The earth, our home, is beginning to look more and more like an immense pile of filth. In many parts of the planet, the elderly lament that once beautiful landscapes are now covered with rubbish.'[4] He gives pride of place to Patriarch Bartholomew of Constantinople, the leader of 300 million Orthodox Christians. For the first time in a papal encyclical there is a reference to his fellow Jesuit the paleontologist Pierre Teilhard de Chardin, although he could not quite bring himself to quote him. He does quote the Protestant Paul Ricoeur who wrote 'I express myself in expressing the world; in my effort to decipher the sacredness of the world, I explore my own'[5]. Encyclicals characteristically end with a prayer composed by the Pope. We are given two prayers: one for Christians and one for all believers. This is a pope wanting to reach out to all persons who have a care for the environment and for the poor, regardless of their religious affiliations. Remember this is the pope who when meeting with the international press corps after his election as pope, told said:

> I told you I was cordially imparting my blessing. Since many of you
> are not members of the Catholic Church, and others are not believers,
> I cordially give this blessing silently, to each of you, respecting the

---

3. *Laudato Si'*, 16.
4. *Laudato Si'*, 21.
5. *Laudato Si'*, 85.

conscience of each, but in the knowledge that each of you is a child of God. May God bless you![6]

Now that is what I call a real blessing for anybody and everybody—and not a word of Vaticanese. Respect for the conscience of every person, regardless of their religious beliefs; silence in the face of difference; affirmation of the dignity and blessedness of every person; offering, not coercing; suggesting, not dictating; leaving room for gracious acceptance.

His concerns are not narrowly dogmatic or pedagogical but universally pastoral. He knows that millions of people, including erstwhile Catholics, are now suspicious of or not helped by notions of tradition, authority, ritual and community when it comes to their own spiritual growth which is now more individual and eclectic. He wants to step beyond the Church's perceived lack of authenticity and its moral focus on individual matters, more often than not, sexual. He thinks the world is in a mess, particularly with the state of the planet—climate change, loss of biodiversity and water shortages, and with the oppression of the poor whose life basics are not assured by the operation of the free market, and with the clutter and violence of lives which are cheated of the opportunity for interior peace. At the conclusion of the encyclical he describes the document as a 'lengthy reflection which has been both joyful and troubling'.[7] He is going to great pains to demystify his office and to demystify papal documents. Clearly he wants all people of good will to emulate him and to be both joyful and troubled as they wrestle with the problems of the age.

Why Would Pope Francis have Something to Say About Climate Change?

Francis thinks the planet risks going to hell in a basket. He says he is 'pointing to the cracks in the planet'.[8] Perhaps we should take heart from Leonard Cohen's observation, 'There is a crack in everything. That's how the light gets in'. This is the only home we have. And the

---

6. Pope Francis, Address to Members of Communications Media, at <http://w2.vatican.va/content/francesco/en/speeches/2013/march/documents/papa-francesco_20130316_rappresentanti-media.html>. Accessed 16 March 2013.
7. Pope Francis, *Laudato Si'*, 246.
8. *Laudato Si'*, 163.

science is in. It indicates that climate change is real. The loss of bio-diversity is real. Human activity continues to contribute adversely to both changes, though of course there are other causes. We cannot undo the other causes. We do have the power to change and to address some of the human causes. An untrammeled free market will not provide the solution, neither will untrammeled governments, whether they be self-seeking and corrupt or populist and short sighted. Francis sees an urgent need for people to be well educated, to be concerned about future generations, and to be focused beyond their national borders. He sees an urgent need for governments to abide by the rule of law. He sees an urgent need for markets to be regulated so that self-interest and economic imperatives can be better aligned to pay dividends for the planet and for future generations. He doesn't see how this can be done unless more people, especially those designing laws and regulations for government and economic actors, are integrated in themselves, finding completion in a deep interior life marked by concern for neighbor, and for creation as well as self. Francis calls us to consider the tragic effects of environmental degradation, especially on the lives of the world's poorest. He says:

> The problem is that we still lack the culture needed to confront this crisis. We lack leadership capable of striking out on new paths and meeting the needs of the present with concern for all and without prejudice towards coming generations. The establishment of a legal framework which can set clear boundaries and ensure the protection of ecosystems has become indispensable, otherwise the new power structures based on the techno-economic paradigm may overwhelm not only our politics but also freedom and justice.[9]

Developing the culture, the leadership, and the legal framework. These are the challenges to those of us who want to be intelligent believers responding to the call of the Spirit. Having noted, 'There are certain environmental issues where it is not easy to achieve a broad consensus', he concedes that 'the Church does not presume to settle scientific questions or to replace politics'. He continues, 'but I want to encourage an honest and open debate, so that particular interests or ideologies will not prejudice the common good'.[10]

---

9. *Laudato Si'*, 53.
10. *Laudato Si'*, 188.

Hailing from Argentina, he puts his trust neither in ideological Communism nor in unbridled capitalism. Like his predecessors Benedict and John Paul II he is unapologetic when asserting, '[b]y itself the market cannot guarantee integral human development and social inclusion.'[11] His concern is not to settle arguments about politics, economics or science. He makes no pretence to give the last word on anything. He is not even much concerned to give the last word on scriptural interpretation or theological insights into topics such as anthropocentrism. He is wanting to enliven the passion and the spiritual commitment of his readers who, grasping the link between care for the earth, care for the poor, and care for the personal interior life, will be motivated to work for real change.

What New Ideas are to be Found in Pope Francis's Letter?

Francis calls everyone to engagement in an honest and open debate, respecting the competencies of all, and inspired by the vision of St Francis of Assisi who is the model of the inseparable bond 'between concern for nature, justice for the poor, commitment to society, and interior peace'[12].

There are probably no genuinely new ideas in the encyclical. Like many, he is convinced that we need to phase out our reliance on fossil fuels—coal, oil, 'and to a lesser degree, gas'—progressively and without delay.[13] He thinks any scheme for buying and selling carbon credits is deeply flawed.[14] He is a great advocate for solar energy.[15] But what is new is the integration of the scientific, the political, the sociological, the spiritual and the theological – an integration given the stamp of approval of the leader of one of the world's most significant religious communities. Granted that the Judeo-Christian tradition has done much to inculcate the notion that we humans are to subdue the earth, it is heartening that a pope has been able to say:

> The best way to restore men and women to their rightful place, putting an end to their claim to absolute dominion over the earth, is to speak once more of the figure of a Father who creates and who alone

---

11. *Laudato Si'*, 109.
12. *Laudato Si'*, 11.
13. *Laudato Si'*, 165.
14. *Laudato Si'*, 171.
15. *Laudato Si'*, 172.

owns the world. Otherwise, human beings will always try to impose their own laws and interests on reality.[16]

It could be even more helpful for us to move beyond the patriarchal view of God. It is not only the Church that has been complicit, but it has been complicit especially in ventures of colonisation aimed at plundering the resources of indigenous peoples. Francis notes, that 'modernity has been marked by an excessive anthropocentrism'.[17] The New Testament treatment in the encyclical is a little light-on. I think evangelical Protestants would do better here. But he does draw a good colloquid-permitted lesson from the Old Testament creation accounts noting:

> The sheer novelty involved in the emergence of a personal being within a material universe presupposes a direct action of God and a particular call to life and to relationship on the part of a 'Thou' who addresses himself to another 'thou'. The biblical accounts of creation invite us to see each human being as a subject who can never be reduced to the status of an object.18

Those in our pews who would not count themselves as being too religious might garner the same sense by recalling the stuttering Gemmy in the opening of David Malouf's *Remembering Babylon* when he calls out, 'Do not shoot. I am a B-b-british object!' Where I find Francis truly prophetic, and this is where he grates on the Murdoch press and the conservative Catholic think tanks in the United States of America, is in his bold declaration:

> If we acknowledge the value and the fragility of nature and, at the same time, our God-given abilities, we can finally leave behind the modern myth of unlimited material progress. A fragile world, entrusted by God to human care, challenges us to devise intelligent ways of directing, developing and limiting our power.[19]

Of course, the real heresy of this pope in the eyes of the free marketeers who long presumed that the anti-Communist Polish Pope John

---

16. *Laudato Si'*, 75.
17. *Laudato Si'*, 116.
18. *Laudato Si'*, 81.
19. *Laudato Si'*, 78.

Paul II was their unswerving ally is that he speaks of the need first to 'reject a magical conception of the market'[20] and then to redefine 'our notion of progress'.[21] He proceeds to utter the unthinkable, that 'the time has come to accept decreased growth in some parts of the world, in order to provide resources for other places to experience healthy growth'[22]. This papal prescription is very difficult to reconcile with Christine Lagarde's oft repeated IMF claim that what the world, and most especially the poor need, is strong economic growth across the board internationally. For example, Lagarde when speaking on 'Decisive Action to Secure Durable Growth' in April 2016 claimed: 'From a macroeconomic perspective, the first priority must be to secure the recovery and lay the foundation for stronger and more equitable medium-term growth. Overcoming the voices of despair and exclusion requires an alternative path—one that leads to prospects for more employment, higher incomes, and more secure lives.'[23]

There are still fundamental disagreements about the most basic issues underpinning sustainable, equitable economic wellbeing for all, including the requirement for continued economic growth and the necessity of reducing greenhouse gas emissions and other human contributions to the warming of the planet. Pope Francis could well have had some of our Jesuit educated Australian Cabinet ministers in mind when he wrote:

A politics concerned with immediate results, supported by consumerist sectors of the population, is driven to produce short-term growth. In response to electoral interests, governments are reluctant to upset the public with measures which could affect the level of consumption or create risks for foreign investment. The myopia of power politics delays the inclusion of a far-sighted environmental agenda within the overall agenda of governments. Thus we forget that "time is greater than space", that we are always more effective when we generate processes rather than holding on to positions of power. True statecraft is manifest when, in difficult times, we uphold high principles and think

20. *Laudato Si'*, 190.
21. *Laudato Si'*, 194.
22. *Laudato Si'*, 193.
23. Christine Lagarde, 'Decisive Action to Secure Durable Growth', (Bundesbank and Goethe University Frankfurt, Germany), available at <https://www.imf.org/external/np/speeches/2016/040516.htm>. Accessed 5 April 2016.

of the long-term common good. Political powers do not find it easy to assume this duty in the work of nation-building.[24]

In October 2015, the *New York Times* columnist Andrew Revkin spoke in Brisbane at the Global Integrity Summit. He has been writing about science and the environment for more than three decades. Through his hard-hitting coverage of global warming he has earned most of the major awards for science journalism. He is no papal groupie but he reported on being one of the experts called to Rome for consultations when the encyclical was being drafted. In his Brisbane presentation, Revkin particularly emphasized this paragraph from the encyclical:

> [W]e need to acknowledge that different approaches and lines of thought have emerged regarding this situation and its possible solutions. At one extreme, we find those who doggedly uphold the myth of progress and tell us that ecological problems will solve themselves simply with the application of new technology and without any need for ethical considerations or deep change. At the other extreme are those who view men and women and all their interventions as no more than a threat, jeopardizing the global ecosystem, and consequently the presence of human beings on the planet should be reduced and all forms of intervention prohibited. Viable future scenarios will have to be generated between these extremes, since there is no one path to a solution. This makes a variety of proposals possible, all capable of entering into dialogue with a view to developing comprehensive solutions.[25]

Revkin was impressed at Francis's willingness to listen attentively to all views and to weigh the evidence. But we are left wondering whether Francis does take sides or not on the desirability of arresting economic growth at least in some countries and of taking drastic action to reduce human impacts on the climate.

In his folksy style, Francis notes that 'sobriety and humility were not favourably regarded in the last century'.[26] He calls us back to a 'serene attentiveness',[27] reminding us in a grandfatherly way 'that being

---

24. *Laudato Si'*, #178.
25. *Laudato Si'*, 60.
26. *Laudato Si'*, 224.
27. *Laudato Si'*, 226.

good and decent are worth it'.[28] Following the lead of the Australian bishops, he calls us to an 'ecological conversion', having a go at those 'committed and prayerful Christians [who], with the excuse of realism and pragmatism, tend to ridicule expressions of concern for the environment.'[29]

The encyclical would be all the stronger if it conceded that the growth in the world's human population—from two billion when Pius XII first spoke of contraception to 3.5 billion when Paul VI promulgated *Humanae Vitae* to 7.4 billion and climbing as it is today—points to a need to reconsider the Church's teaching on contraception. The pope is quite right to insist that the reduction of population growth is not the only solution to the environmental crisis. But it is part of the solution. It may even be an essential part of the solution. Banning contraception in a world of 7.4 billion people confronting the challenges of climate change and loss of biodiversity is a very different proposition from banning it in a world of only two billion people oblivious of such challenges. I don't think you would find any papal advisers today who would advocate that the planet's situation with climate change, loss of biodiversity, and water shortages would be improved if only all people of good will had declined to use artificial birth control for the last fifty years.

Joy filled and troubled, Francis is inviting us to do something to change the market settings and political settings here in Australia to modify the behaviour of all Australians in the future, and he invites us to attend to our own Franciscan interior ecological conversion with our care for the vulnerable and 'an integral ecology lived out joyfully and authentically'[30]. For starters, I should probably start rejoicing each time I catch the Murrays coach from Canberra to Sydney rather than the Qantas jet, regardless of who is paying. Even in the middle of the Canberra winter, I should also take to heart the Pope's observation, 'A person who could afford to spend and consume more but regularly uses less heating and wears warmer clothes, shows the kind of convictions and attitudes which help to protect the environment.'[31] Caring for our common home begins at home. But

---

28. *Laudato Si'*, 229.
29. *Laudato Si'*, 217.
30. *Laudato Si'*, 10.
31. *Laudato Si'*, 211.

that's only the beginning, and it will get us nowhere unless there is agreement and committed action posited on economic growth tailored to the wellbeing of the poorest, economic activity within markets and state regulation designed to reduce the human impact on global warming.

The Economic Credibility of Pope Francis: *The Australian* newspaper and *Laudato Si'*

Bruce Duncan

Introduction

The economic views of Pope Francis have been sharply contested, particularly by special interest groups and advocates of the neoliberal economic policies that he so consistently critiques. Such reactions are to be expected, of course, and deserve careful scrutiny. Some more sympathetic economists have also raised questions about how well or accurately Francis has expressed in economic terms his concerns about eradicating poverty and hunger, and reducing inequality.[1]

The Australian newspaper in a number of articles trenchantly criticised the 2015 encyclical of Pope Francis, *Laudato Si': On care for our common home*, as wrong about climate change and ignorant about economics. *The Australian's* editor-at-large, Paul Kelly, on 24 June 2015 declared the Pope's language was 'almost hysterical. Profound intellectual ignorance is dressed up as honouring God.'

'Page after page reveals Francis and his advisers as environmental populists and economic ideologues of a quasi-Marxist bent.' He wrote that the Pope has 'delegitimised as immoral' pro-market economic forces. As for Tony Abbott and his Catholic backers, this is a 'relentless repudiation of their ethical framework and policies'.

Kelly alleged that the Pope is totally opposed to the market mechanism and ignorant about the great uplift in living standards in many countries. 'Francis is blind to the liberating power of markets and technology'. It is a 'pure green view of economic and human progress' that calls for decreased growth and opposes maximisation of prof-

---

1. Joseph Kaboski, 'The Pope doesn't Care about Capitalism', 31 August 2015, CNBC, at http://www.cnbc.com/he-pope-doesnt-care-about-capitalism-commentary.html. Accessed 31 August 2015.

its. 'His message fits perfectly with reactionary dogma now gospel in Catholic schools throughout Australia.'[2]

Kelly seriously misrepresented *Laudato Si'*, surprisingly so for such a senior journalist and economic commentator. Contrary to Kelly's allegation that the Pope is 'blind to the liberating power of markets and technology', Pope Francis explicitly acknowledges and rejoices in the benefits of modern science, technology and creativity which have resulted in advances for humankind (*Laudato Si'* 102). 'In order to continue providing employment, it is imperative to promote an economy which favours productive diversity and business creativity . . . Business is a noble vocation, directed to producing wealth and improving our world' (129). Francis well knows that economic growth is needed to lift millions more out of poverty, but he is calling urgently for greater equity and sustainability, with less waste and more moderate consumption.

Kelly has long been a strident critic of the Church's social teaching, particularly about the morality of markets. In *The Australian* on 26 October 2005 he wrote:

> The intellectual failure of the churches to accept the moral foundations of a market economy and market-based mechanisms to deliver equity dooms them to a historic marginalisation. When on earth will the Catholic Church emerge from the defeatist and myopic economics of BA Santamaria? When will it discover one of the elementary precepts of the 18th century, namely the moral laws built into economic liberalism?[3]

The 1400-word editorial of *The Australian* on 27–28 June 2015, 'Papal prescription for a flawed economic order', added that Pope Francis 'appears to have swallowed a new pernicious dogma' and denounced free-market principles in the guise of 'religious instruction'. The editorial vehemently disapproved of the Pope's warnings of catastrophic climate change. The Pope's 'outburst betrays a fundamental ignorance of economic history', and given his influence, his views could

---

2.   Paul Kelly, 'Green-Left Pope Endorses Flawed View of Progress', *The Australian,* 24 June, 2015. I have found no public comment on *Laudato Si'* from Tony Abbott, presumably because he does not agree with Pope Francis on these issues of climate change and economics.

3.   Paul Kelly, 'Half-Measures Could Thwart Equity Goals', *The Australian,* 26 October 2005, 16.

hurt the poor. It alleged that Francis wanted to 'extend this new form of bureaucratic tyranny to his main economic imperative, re-slicing the economic pie, not enlarging it.'

The editorial continued that 'Francis has stepped over important demarcations between church and state, blurring the lines between God and Caesar… And turbocharging the UN and other agencies as secular theocracies, even under papal approval, would impair human progress.'[4]

Again, this gravely misrepresented what the Pope said; he envisaged freely agreed systems of international governance to face major world problems, not a tyranny. And far from overstepping demarcations between church and state, Francis urged productive dialogue among all parties to solve problems of poverty and injustice. He does not offer solutions or blueprints. He specifically states that 'different approaches and lines of thought have emerged regarding this situation and its possible solutions.' Many approaches are possible, 'all capable of entering into dialogue' (LS 60). 'On many concrete questions, the Church has no reason to offer a definitive opinion; she knows that honest debate must be encouraged among experts, while respecting divergent views. But we need only take a frank look at the facts to see that our common home is falling into serious disrepair' (LS 61).

In addition, far from wanting to see the pie sliced and diced, the Pope was urging smarter growth, lifting millions more out of poverty, with much less extreme concentrations of wealth certainly, but in an environmentally responsible way to ensure adequate resources for current and future generations. So that other parts of the world could experience healthy growth, he did say it was time 'to accept decreased growth in some parts of the world', because of overconsumption there (LS 193).

A phalanx of The Australian's writers joined the attack on the encyclical. Angela Shanahan quoted Fr James Grant, adjunct fellow at the Institute of Public Affairs, that the encyclical 'should not be treated as official Catholic doctrine' but as a personal opinion of the Pope, and so 'Catholics can feel safe in being sceptical about the Pope's opinions.'[5] Tess Livingstone wrote that Catholics were not bound to

---

4. Editorial, 'Papal Prescription for a Flawed Economic Order: the Church Should Not Belong to the Green-Left Fringe', The Australian, 27–28 June 2015, 23.
5. Angela Shanahan, 'Francis's Encyclical on Climate Change isn't the Gospel Truth for Catholics', The Australian, 20–21 June 2015.

accept Pope Francis's views on climate change, and that his views on markets will make his economic prescriptions 'largely irrelevant'.[6]

Nick Cater of the Menzies Research Centre declared that 'Francis the Handwringer' was 'so overcome with gloom that he makes the prophet Job look cheery'.[7] Gerard Henderson advised all 'not to regard *Laudato Si'* as in any sense infallible'.[8] At least Archbishop Denis Hart was given room to endorse the encyclical.[9] *The Australian* was unexpectedly provocative and one-sided in its attacks on the encyclical. It would appear that the Pope had challenged sensitive economic assumptions of the paper and its political allies.

The Australian newspaper did not allow any rejoinder to these articles, or even barely a letter to the editor in reply. I submitted a response but the paper did not accept it; instead it was published by *Eureka Street* on 9 July. I pointed out that Paul Kelly and the editorial were making very serious allegations against the Pope; in effect they were arguing that he was recklessly misrepresenting Catholic social teaching and was grossly incompetent not only in economics but as a church leader.[10]

Brian Lawrence, chair of the Australian Catholic Council of Employment Relations and an authority on industrial issues and Catholic social teaching, wrote a detailed response to *The Australian*, showing how many of the quotations from the Pope were taken out of context, were 'unjustified and grossly unfair'.[11] *The Australian* alleged that Francis 'appears to have swallowed a new, pernicious dogma . . . of the anti-free market global green movement.' Lawrence

---

6. Tess Livingstone, 'Pope Turns Left on the Environment', *The Australian*, 20–21 June 2015.

7. Nick Cater, 'The Wretched Gospel of Pope Francis the Handwringer', *The Australian*, 23 June 2015.

8. Gerard Henderson, 'The Pope can have his Climate Change Say, but it is No Hard and Fast Rule' *The Australian*, 27–28 June 2015.

9. Denis Hart, 'Francis Inspires Us to Care for our World and for Others', *The Australian*, 27–28 June 2015.

10. Bruce Duncan, 'The Australian Gangs up on Pope Francis', *Eureka Street*, at http://www.eurekastreet.com.au/article.aspx?aeid=45203#.VufcDEByK4M, accessed 9 July 2015.

11. Brian Lawrence, 'The Economics of Laudato Si': No Surprises Here', Australian Catholic Council for Employment Relations, at http://www.accer.asn.au/index.php/papers/134-the-economics-of-laudato-si-no-surprises-here/file, 2. Accessed 14 September 2015.

regarded this as a 'slur' that implied the Pope's views were not part of Catholic social teaching. Lawrence showed that Francis is in solid agreement with his papal predecessors, especially Popes John Paul II and Benedict XVI, both in relation to concern for the environment and their critique of the ideology behind the neoliberal version of free markets.[12]

Other Critics of Francis's Economic Views

Stephen Stromberg in the *Washington Post* of 18 June wrote that Francis's warning about trading in carbon credits gave the impression that he was opposed to 'cap and trade' schemes that used the market to minimise carbon emissions in the most economically efficient manner. Stromberg noted that the US had effectively used a cap-and-trade system to reduce acid rain, but added that perhaps the Pope was referring to the European Union's 'incompetently designed' system. 'Carbon pricing would do exactly what Francis professes to want . . . if properly calibrated.'[13]

In the *New York Times* Joseph Heathjune critiqued *Laudato Si'* for criticising carbon credits, alleging that the Pope said the environment 'cannot be "safeguarded by market forces"'. The scepticism of Pope Francis about market-based solutions was based on a misunderstanding, Heathjune wrote, and that both carbon taxes and emissions trading 'reflected moral conviction.'[14]

In *Fortune* magazine Chris Matthews quoted Robert N Stavins, director of the environmental economics program at Harvard, that the Pope was favouring an approach of a 'small set of socialist Latin American countries that are opposed to the world economic order, fearful of free markets, and have been utterly dismissive and uncooperative in the international climate negotiations.'[15]

---

12. Lawrence, 'The Economics of *Laudato Si'*, 33.
13. Stephen Stromberg, 'What Pope Francis Gets Wrong about Climate Change', *Washington Post*, https://www.washingtonpost.com/blogs/post-partisan/wp/2015/06/18/what-pope-francis-gets-wrong-about-climate-change/. Accessed 18 June 2015.
14. Joseph Heathjune, 'Pope Francis' Climate Error', *New York Times* http://www.nytimes.com/2015/06/20/opinion/pope-francis-climate-error.html?_r=0. Accessed 19 June 2015.
15. Chris Matthews, 'Even Liberals Think the Pope Needs an Economics Lesson', *Fortune*, at http://fortune.com/2015/09/23/pope-francis-climate-change-liberals. Accessed 23 September 2015.

Some Catholic groups were also critical of papal rejection of neoliberal economics. The Catholic neoconservatives, George Weigel, Richard Neuhaus and Michael Novak have consistently tried to reinterpret Catholic social thought in a way more acceptable to United States right-wing political and economic interests. As Michael Sean Winters wrote, 'Novak's writings embody the most strident defense of the modern economic system Pope Francis denounces. Neuhaus has gone to God but his journal, *First Things*, has become the house organ for opposition to Francis.'[16]

Robert George wrote in *First Things* on 3 January 2015 that whatever the Pope said on climate change could be ignored since he was not an expert. And two days later, Maureen Mullarkey in a blog added that the Pope was an 'ideologue' and a 'parasite' who 'sullied his office' with his 'theologized propaganda'. *First Things* later disowned the blog.[17] A writer from the Action Institute, Dr Samuel Gregg, told the *Business Spectator* that the Pope's document was 'in many respects . . . a caricature of market economics.'[18] He wrote that 'it's lamentable that this pontificate seems so unwilling to engage in a serious discussion about the market economy's moral and economic merits.'[19]

In Australia, Merv Bendle in *Quadrant* magazine accused the Pope of appearing 'to capitulate to the neo-Marxist paganism that underlines the Deep Green ideology'. The encyclical was 'economically illiterate, perpetuating the myth that poverty can be overcome through moral exhortation, central control and income redistribution, rather than the promotion of free enterprise and individual effort.' It was a 're-hash of the familiar Marxist-Leninist diatribes against Western imperialism', as the Pope 'proposes that this murderous and dicta-

---

16. Michael Sean Winters, 'Review: a Partisan Church III', *National Catholic Reporter*, http://ncronline.org/blogs/distinctly-catholic/review-partisan-church-part-iii. Accessed 2 July 2015.

17. Damon Linker, 'Republican Party's War with Pope Francis has finally Started', *The Week*, http://theweek.com/articles/532784/republican-partys-warwith-pope-francishas-finally-started. Accessed 13 January 2015.

18. Quoted in Michael Sean Winters, 'Laudato Si' – Magistra No', in *National Catholic Reporter*, 19 June, 2015.

19. Samuel Gregg, '*Laudato Si*': Well Intentioned, Economically Flawed', *The American Spectator*, http://spectator.org/articles/63160/laudato-si%E2%80%99-well-intentioned-economically-flawed. Accessed 19 June 2016.

torial approach be pursued on a global scale, using the notoriously corrupt United Nations as its vehicle or model.'[20]

Let us take up the issue of the Pope's attack on the neoliberal version of free-market ideology first, then consider the economic expertise behind the encyclical, the issues of carbon trading and speculation, and finally the credibility and moral authority of *Laudato Si'*.

Free Market

The Australian is correct that the encyclical is indeed a trenchant repudiation of the neoliberal economics that has dominated various conservative circles in recent years. Such a strong repudiation by the Pope is not new in Catholic social thinking; it developed over a century in papal encyclicals. Even John Paul II in his celebrated *Centesimus Annus* (1991) after the collapse of the Soviet Union attacked 'unbridled capitalism' which upheld 'the absolute predominance of capital' over labour and society.

> In the struggle against such a system, what is being proposed as an alternative is not the socialist system, which in fact turns out to be State capitalism, but rather *a society of free work, of enterprise and of participation*. Such a society is not directed against the market, but demands that the market be appropriately controlled by the forces of society and by the State, so as to guarantee that the basic needs of the whole of society are satisfied.[21]

John Paul II warned that after the collapse of communism 'a radical capitalist ideology could spread', blindly entrusting societies to unregulated free market forces.[22] He repeatedly criticised 'neoliberal' capitalism in particular, saying in Latvia in 1993 that the Church had 'always distanced itself from capitalist ideology, holding it responsible for grave social injustices'.[23] In Cuba in 1998 he again

---

20. Merv Bendle, 'An Apostate Pope?', *Quadrant Online*, at < https://quadrant.org. au/opinion/doomed-planet/2015/07/apostate-pope/.> Accessed 15 July 2015.
21. Pope John Paul II, *Centesimus Annus*, 1 May 1991, #33, at < http://w2.vatican.va/ content/john-paul-ii/en/encyclicals/documents/hf_jp-ii_enc_01051991_cen-tesimus-annus.html.> Accessed 1 May 1991.
22. John Paul II, *Centesimus Annus*, #33.
23. John Paul II, 'What Catholic Social Teaching is and is Not', in *Origins* 23/15 (23 September 1993): 257.

attacked 'a certain capitalist neoliberalism that subordinates the human person to blind market forces', and places 'intolerable burdens' on poorer countries.[24]

Following the Synod of Bishops of the Americas in 1999, John Paul wrote that 'a system known as "neoliberalism" prevails; based on a purely economic conception of man, this system considers profit and the law of the market as its only parameters, to the detriment of the dignity of and the respect due to individuals and peoples.'[25]

Likewise, Benedict XVI warned against growing inequality and 'ruinous exploitation of the planet'. Writing in the aftermath of the Global Financial Crisis, Benedict's 2009 encyclical *Caritas in Veritate* insisted that economic activity must consider the wellbeing of all, and not just accumulate wealth apart from considerations of social and distributive justice.[26]

In short, the Global Financial Crisis exposed the ethical crisis in modern economics, especially in its neoliberal form. The Church has never opposed the market in principle but insisted that it be well-regulated to ensure social justice for all involved, workers, investors, business people and the wider community alike. Neoliberal thinkers, on the other hand, have tried to reduce regulation and constraints on business as much as possible, in the belief that markets will almost automatically produce the most efficient, and hence most moral, outcomes.

Pope Francis, of course, recognises the great advances in living standards in many countries since the Second World War, but laments that finance capital and global corporations are changing the rules so that wealth is pouring into the coffers of the very rich while whole populations are left struggling.[27]

---

24. John Paul II, 25 January 1998, quoted in John Sniegocki, *Catholic Social Teaching and Economic Globalization: The Quest for Alternatives* (Milwaukee WI: Marquette University Press, 2009), 148.
25. John Paul II, Apostolic Exhortation *Ecclesia in America*, 22, #56 at <http://w2.vatican.va/content/john-paul-ii/en/apost_exhortations/documents/hf_jp-ii_exh_22011999_ecclesia-in-america.html> Accessed 22 January 1999.
26. Pope Benedict XVI, *Caritas in Veritate*, 29, #36, at <http://w2.vatican.va/content/benedict-xvi/en/encyclicals/documents/hf_ben-xvi_enc_20090629_caritas-in-veritate.html.> Accessed 29 June 2009. For some of Benedict's statements on the environment, see Lawrence, 'The Economics of Laudato Si', 21–22.
27. Gerard O'Connell, 'Pope Francis: To Care for the Poor is Not Communism, It is the Gospel', at *America Magazine*, <http://www.americamagazine.org/content/dispatches/pope-francis-care-poor-not-communism-it-gospel > Accessed 11 January 2015.

Francis constantly pleads for investors and business people to develop economic activity that will more quickly eradicate hunger and the worst poverty, increase living standards and opportunity more broadly, and restrain excessive consumption to secure a more equitable and sustainable future.[28]

The Pope is especially speaking for hundreds of millions of people in the developing world, protesting against the unfairness in economic outcomes, the despoliation of their resources and environment, and the fact that their peoples will be hit hardest by the effects of global warming. Through its very extensive networks in developing countries, the Church is well aware of the looming threats to people's wellbeing.

The Economic Critique by Pope Francis

Francis has made no secret of his attack on neoliberalism and its economic implications. The popes have long objected to 'unrestrained capitalism' or 'economic liberalism' that manipulated the global economy to serve dominant special interests. Francis wrote in his 2013 document, *The Joy of the Gospel,* that the 'trickle-down' theories that were supposed to promote wellbeing for everyone have proved naïve and delusive because of the failure in moral underpinnings. (54) 'A new tyranny is born, invisible and often virtual, which unilaterally and relentlessly imposes its own laws and rules.' (56).[29] Francis insisted that his critique is 'the inescapable social dimension of the Gospel message.' (258). 'You cannot serve both God and money'. In his words of 20 September 2013, this 'was not communism! This is pure Gospel!'[30]

Pope Francis was closely involved in the writing of *Laudato Si'* and insisted that reform of capitalism, global warming and sustainability are among the most urgent moral issues of our time. He wants to help mobilise not just Catholics but all people of good will in raising consciousness and urging everyone to act as responsible guardians of the environment and resources for coming generations.

---

28. Pope Francis, *The Joy of the Gospel: Apostolic Exhortation on the Proclamation of the Gospel in Today's World,* (24 November 2013), #203.
29. See also Bruce Duncan, 'Pope Francis's Call for Social Justice in the Global Economy', *Australasian Catholic Record,* 91/2 (April 2014): 178–94.
30. Pope Francis, *L'Osservatore Romano,* 21 September 2013.

As the new cardinal of Buenos Aires he witnessed Argentina collapse into poverty during the economic crisis of 2001–2 as his country plunged into the largest financial default in history till that time. From being a comparatively prosperous country with only four per cent of the people living in poverty in 1990, in 2001 half the population fell below the poverty line, banks collapsed, many lost their life savings and 40,000 businesses failed. Bergoglio helped marshal church and community groups into emergency support networks.[31]

Bergoglio was one of the most important leaders at the meeting of the bishops of Latin America at Aparecida in Brazil in 2007, and supervised the writing of its 160-page report, summarising their protests against extreme economic inequality and the damaging effects of neoliberal economic policies in their countries.[32] The Global Financial Crisis was an extension on a global basis of much of what Bergoglio had already seen in Argentina and elsewhere in Latin America.

Pope Francis was particularly forthright during his trips to Latin America, where he is very familiar with the economic and social problems of the majority of the people. In Bolivia in July 2015 he attacked the single-minded pursuit of money as an idol, quoting one of the early Church Fathers, Basil of Caesarea, who described greed for money as 'the dung of the devil'. Francis continued: 'An unfettered pursuit of money rules . . . The service of the common good is left behind . . . once greed for money presides over the entire socioeconomic system, it ruins society, it condemns and enslaves men and women.'[33]

Expertise Behind the Encyclical

Laudato Si' develops the Pope's own moral critique, but he has consulted widely, including with many eminent specialists, notably through the Pontifical Council for Justice and Peace which worked closely with experts in the Pontifical Academy of Social Sciences, formerly headed by the Harvard Law Professor Mary Ann Glendon; the Pontifical Academy of Sciences, with almost 40 Nobel laureates

---

31. Paul Vallely, *Pope Francis: Untying the Knots* (London: Bloomsbury, 2013), 116.
32. *The Aparecida Document: Fifth General Conference of the Bishops of Latin America and the Caribbean* (Lexington KY: 2007).
33. Pope Francis, Address to the Popular Movements, 9 Santa Cruz, Bolivia <http://w2.vatican.va/content/francesco/en/speeches/2015/july/documents/papa-francesco_20150709_bolivia-movimenti-popolari.html> Accessed 9 July 2015.

among its members; the Vatican Secretariat of State with its extensive diplomatic network and resources, as well as drawing from the concerns of episcopal conferences around the world.

The Pope himself has met many of the leading specialists and economists, including Joseph Stiglitz and Amartya Sen, along with numerous world leaders including Barack Obama and the United Nations Secretary General, Ban Ki-moon, both of whom welcomed the encyclical enthusiastically, especially in view of the forthcoming world conferences on climate change.

Stiglitz has had significant influence among papal advisers, particularly on Monsignor Marcelo Sanchez Sorondo, chancellor of both the Pontifical Academy of Science and the Pontifical Academy of Social Sciences. Stiglitz was appointed to the Pontifical Academy of Social Sciences in 2003.[34]

Stiglitz wrote the famous article in March 2011 in *Vanity Fair,* 'Of the 1%, by the 1%, for the 1%', that demonstrated the extreme and increasing inequality in the United States, and sparked the 'Occupy Wall Street' movement. In many books, he has shown how in the United States of America most of the wealth has gone to the top income groups, and the great bulk of the population has hardly benefited at all over recent decades. The top one per cent has accumulated astronomical wealth, unimaginable in earlier generations, and with that has come unprecedented political influence and power.

In his 2010 book *Freefall* Stiglitz lamented that 'too little has been written about the underlying "moral deficit" that has been exposed [by the] unrelenting pursuit of profits and elevation of the pursuit of self-interest.'[35]

That those policies had been shaped by special interests—of the financial markets—is obvious. More complex is the role of economics. Among the long list of those to blame for the crisis, I would include the economics profession, for it provided the special interests with arguments about efficient and self-regulating markets—even though

---

34. Alejandro Chafuen, 'Pope Francis and the Economists', *Forbes,* 4 December 2013. Free-market economists of the Chicago School have also been represented on the Pontifical Academy of Science, including Gary Becker, from 1997.
35. Joseph E Stiglitz, *Freefall: America, Free Markets, and the Sinking of the World Economy* (New York: WW Norton, 2010), 278.

advances in economics during the preceding two decades had shown the limited conditions under which that theory held true.[36]

In *The Price of Inequality* (2012) Stiglitz added that 'while globalization may benefit society as a whole, it has left many behind—not a surprise given that, to a large extent, globalization has been managed by corporate and other special interests for their benefit.'[37]

In *Rewriting the Rules of the American Economy: an Agenda for Growth and Shared Prosperity* (2016), Stiglitz summarised his critique of globalisation and the power of international finance in the way the economy has benefited the very rich at the expense of the great majority of Americans.

In recent decades, 'the benefits of economic growth have disproportionately gone to the top twenty per cent of the population while the share of national income going to the bottom ninety-nine percent has fallen. Incomes, especially for men, have stagnated during this time . . . We now know that developed economies can rise without lifting all boats.'[38] He blamed the supply-side economic theories 'driven by conservative ideology and special interests' that led to US policymakers deregulating the economy.[39] His book is a scathing indictment of the power of special interests, and the resulting collusion in fraud, corruption, manipulation of markets and growing inequality. He called for a revival in United States democracy to rewrite the economic rules so that all citizens can have fair incomes and life opportunities.

One of the architects of the Millennium Development Goals and later director of the Earth Institute at Columbia University, Jeffrey Sachs, was 'unnerved' to have to write his 2011 book *The Price of Civilization: Economics and Ethics after the Fall*. He lamented the 'moral deprivation' underlying the Global Financial Crisis. 'Something wrong happened to the moral compass of so many of the people working in the financial sector and elsewhere.'[40] 'Our greatest national illusion is that a healthy society can be organized around the

---

36. Stiglitz, *Freefall*, xx-xxi.
37. Joseph E Stiglitz, *The Price of Inequality: How Today's Divided Society Endangers our Future* (New York: WW Norton, 2012), 277.
38. Joseph E Stiglitz, *Rewriting the Rules of the American Economy: an Agenda for Growth and Shared Prosperity* (New York: WW Norton, 2016), 6–7.
39. Stiglitz, *Rewriting the Rules*, 17.
40. Jeffrey Sachs, *The Price of Civilization: Economics and Ethics after the Fall* (London: The Bodley Head, 2011), xvii.

single-minded pursuit of wealth . . . Our society has turned harsh, with the elites on Wall Street, in Big Oil, and in Washington among the most irresponsible and selfish of all.'[41]

Stiglitz and Sachs are not alone in believing that the crisis is fundamentally an ethical one. Many other eminent economists think the problem is systemic in neoliberal economics, resulting in growing inequality. Robert J Shiller, Kenneth Arrow, Robert Kuttner, Nouriel Roubini, Stephen Mihm, Tomas Sedlacek, Paul Krugman and Robert Skidelsky among many others, follow in the steps of Amartya Sen and call for a renewal of moral perspective in economics.[42]

In the view of the well known economist, Robert Reich, 'the central choice is not between the 'free market' and government; it is between a market organized for broadly based prosperity and one designed to deliver almost all the gains to a few at the top.'[43]

Astonishingly *The Australian* in its critique of *Laudato Si'* claimed that 'present debates about inequality within rich countries, while of academic interest, remain a footnote in the bigger story of falling global inequality and poverty'. That view would come as startling to many economists greatly concerned about inequality and poverty, in developed economies as well as globally, and mismanagement of the international economy.[44]

Paul Kelly dug up the hoary old chestnut that the encyclical is 'flouting science', 'which has smashed Christianity from the time of Darwin'. The truth is that the Pope was following the firm advice from the overwhelming majority of scientists and governments in most countries, including China, about the dangers of climate change. As Francis wrote: 'A very solid scientific consensus indicates that we are presently witnessing a disturbing warming of the climate system' (*LS* 23). In the view of Lord Nicholas Stern, chair of the Grantham Institute and former chief economist of the World Bank, *Laudato Si'* was 'extraordinarily important and original', linking climate change and poverty as 'the two defining challenges of our generation'.[45]

---

41. Sachs, *The Price of Civilization*, 9.
42. See Bruce Duncan, 'Globalisation and the Morality of Economics', in *Interface: a Forum for Theology in the World* 16/1 (2013): 35–63.
43. Robert B Reich, *Saving Capitalism: for the Many, not the Few* (New York: Alfred A Knopf, 2015), 219.
44. Editorial, 'Papal Prescription for a Flawed Economic Order', *The Australian*, 27-28 June 2015, 23.
45. Megan Cornwell, 'Lord Stern: Pope's Encyclical was "perfectly timed" for UN Climate Summit', London *Tablet*, 11 March 2016.

Kelly appears blind to the consequences of global warming which we are already seeing in extreme weather events, threats to food production, increasing heat waves, and rising sea levels likely to force mass migrations of people.

In defence of the climate science behind the encyclical, Hans Joachim Schellnhuber, director of the Potsdam Institute for Climate Impact Science and a world authority in this area, said 'the science of *Laudato Si'* is watertight'. He was involved with consultations about the encyclical and helped launch it. He also specifically supported the encyclical's critique of inequality, saying it is not just 85 of the richest people in the world who control as much wealth as 3.5 billion others, half the entire population of the earth: 'It's actually 60'.[46]

Carbon Trading and Credits

Attracting special criticism of *Laudato Si'* was Pope Francis's comment that 'the strategy of buying and selling "carbon credits" can lead to a new form of speculation which would not help reduce the emission of polluting gases worldwide. It may simply become a ploy which permits maintaining the excessive consumption of some countries and sectors'. (*LS* 171).

The Australian editorial seriously misinterpreted Francis and misleadingly claimed he 'dismisses carbon trading as "a new form of speculation" that would avoid "the radical change present circumstances require"'.[47]

Francis was not making an in-principle statement against carbon trading. He was warning about fraud and corruption in carbon markets, such as had plagued the European Union with its trading scheme. He warned that carbon trading '*can* [my italics] lead to a new form of speculation' and become 'a ploy which permits maintaining the excessive consumption of some countries'. (*LS* 171–72).

---

46. Inés San Martin, 'Expert Calls the Science behind the Encyclical Watertight', *Crux*, at <http://www.cruxnow.com/church/2015/06/18/expert-calls-the-science-behind-the-papal-encyclical-watertight/>. Accessed 18 June 2015. According to Oxfam, sixty-two people in 2015 controlled as much wealth as half the planet's population. In Australia, Oxfam said, one per cent of the population had as much wealth as the bottom sixty per cent. 'An Economy for the 1%', Oxfam Briefing Paper 210, 18 January 2016, <https://www.oxfam.org.au/wp-content/uploads/2016/01/an-economy-for-the-1-percent.pdf>. Accessed 18 January 2016.
47. Editorial, 'Papal Prescription', *The Australian*, 27–28 June 2015.

Francis of course knows that carbon trading may be very important. He is also concerned that the burden of making carbon reductions would be borne mainly by poorer countries when the rich industrial countries caused most of the problem.

Various economists argue that, in theory at least, carbon trading and other market mechanisms are the cheapest way to reduce emissions without compromising growth. But as Rebecca Pearse points out in *Inside Story*, over the last twenty years carbon markets have suffered from regulatory failures and only achieved marginal outcomes.[48]

Ironically, in Australia it is conservatives who have opposed carbon trading 'because it (potentially) involves government action to limit fossil fuels.' Pearse writes that conservatives tried to delegitimise carbon trading by targeting 'the risk associated with international offsets, the failures of the EU carbon market and the regressive impact of carbon pricing.'

Pearse argues that the Paris conference cannot establish a carbon market that can cut emissions strongly enough: 'the carbon market will become increasingly marginal to the debate as the case for energy market reform develops.' Article Six of the Paris agreement also recommended 'balanced non-market approaches' to reducing emissions. She notes new interest in direct regulation, with the Stockholm Environment Institute developing policies for governments to restrict fossil fuel developments.[49]

Failure of EU Carbon Trading Schemes

Carbon trading alone will fail to reduce emissions to keep global temperatures from rising above two degrees centigrade, according to Steffen Böhm from the University of Exeter. The European Union emission trading scheme failed because of 'fraud, corruption, over-allocation of permits and perverse incentives for carbon offsetting—all contributing to the fact that the price for carbon is so low that nobody cares.' Böhm added that offsetting projects in developing countries were responsible for the expansion of polluting indus-

---

48. Rebecca Pearse, 'After Paris: Where Now for Carbon Pricing?' *Inside Story*, 21 December 2015, http://insidestory.org.au/after-paris-where-now-for-carbon-pricing

49. Pearse, 'After Paris'.

tries and land grabs, resulting in 'fraud, support of monocultures, forest enclosures and forced displacements and evictions of indigenous people from their land'.[50]

Böhm strongly defended Pope Francis's scepticism about the operation of carbon markets in practice. He wrote that the 'market-based agenda was pushed by negotiators from the EU, US, Japan and Brazil and provoked an optimistic response from financial, fossil fuel and other industry interests' at the Carbon Expo in Barcelona in May 2015.

As director of the Essex Sustainability Institute at the University of Essex, Böhm carried out research on the operation of the Clean Development Mechanism (CDM) and concluded that 'governments should exclude carbon markets from international climate negotiations.' As an instance, his study showed that between 2005 and 2013, Gujarat Fluorochemicals Limited was awarded more than fifty-five million carbon offset credits for destroying a greenhouse gas, HFC-23, earning the company more than $US500 million. Perversely the CDM credits created incentives to produce more refrigerant gases so the firm could claim credit for destroying the HFC-23. European companies were able to buy the credits, at the expense of the climate and the local communities in India.

'Researchers and activists have linked this profit-driven logic to the creative accounting, financial fraud, phantom emissions reductions and polluter subsidies that have riddled carbon markets, arguing they cannot be reformed and should be scrapped.' The problems extend to other areas in forestry, wind, biogas and coal. He concluded that 'relying on carbon markets will work against the capacity of governments around the world to end the era of coal, oil and gas.'[51]

Katherine Lake from the University of Melbourne also warned of a 'risk that by using foreign emissions reductions countries could delay the task of decarbonising their own economies.'[52]

50. Steffen Böhm, 'How Emissions Trading at Paris Climate Talks has set us up for Failure', *The Conversation*, at <https://theconversation.com/how-emissions-trading-at-paris-climate-talks-has-set-us-up-for-failure-52319>. Accessed 15 December 2015.
51. Steffen Böhm, 'Even the Pope Gets it – Carbon Markets Won't Fix the Climate', *The Conversation*, at <https://theconversation.com/even-the-pope-gets-it-carbon-markets-wont-fix-the-climate-38950>. Accessed 25 June 2015.
52. Katherine Lake, 'How will Carbon M Help the Paris Climate Agreement?', *The Conversation*, at <https://theconversation.com/how-will-carbon-markets-help-the-paris-climate-agreement-52211>. Accessed 14 December 2015.

Stiglitz himself proposed that a global carbon tax was needed to avoid the free-rider problem, through a common environmental tax on emissions, or a cap and trade policy that set the price of emissions at say eighty dollars a ton.[53]

Speculation

As for speculation, it can be good or bad for economies, as Lawrence Mitchell pointed out in *The Conversation* in November 2014. He defines speculative assets as those having 'little or no identifiable financial substance' but which are intended to be sold at a higher price. This speculation diverts resources away from the productive economy, and becomes 'parasitic', damaging the economy. Mitchell instances stock 'bubbles' where stockholders pressure managers to produce unrealistic short-term increases in stock value and dividends, damaging the long-term productivity of the asset. Mortgage-backed securities provide other instances of investments in derivatives promising unrealistic returns, resulting in an inevitable crash.[54]

According to Joseph Stiglitz and Hamid Rashid, such reckless forms of speculation helped cause the Global Financial Crisis of 2008, and new problems have emerged from the flood of liquidity which has 'disproportionately gone towards creating financial wealth and inflating asset bubbles, rather than strengthening the real economy.' 'When banks are given the freedom to choose, they choose riskless profit or even financial speculation over lending that would support the broader objective of economic growth.' 'The risk of another financial crisis cannot be ignored.'[55]

The Australian economist, Ross Gittins, is also concerned about the speculative market trading of the big banks, and the power and influence of major companies, with their political donations creating the risk of 'policy capture' in Australia.[56] Gittins quotes from John

53. Joseph Stiglitz, 'Carbon Price and Climate Change', <http://carbon-price.com/joseph-stiglitz> Accessed 24 December 2015.
54. Lawrence Mitchell, 'Financial Speculation: the Good, the Bad and the Parasitic', *The Conversation*, <https://theconversation.com/financial-speculation-the-good-the-bad-and-the-parasitic-33613>. Accessed 11 November 2014.
55. Joseph Stiglitz and Hamid Rashid, 'What's Holding Back the World Economy?', *The Guardian,* 9 February 2016.
56. Ross Gittins, 'Rein in the Power Wielded by the Big End of Town', *The Age*, 10 February 2016.

Kay's book, *Other People's Money*, that the massive 'financialisation' by the banks, making extraordinary profits through their speculative activity, is 'socially unproductive' and does not benefit the rest of the economy. He supports splitting the banks so that the speculative banking is totally separate from normal saving and business banking, and that tax payers are not required to rescue speculative banks from failures.[57]

The Credibility and Authority of Pope Francis

The Australian contended that the views in the encyclical are not tenets of faith and morals, and so Catholics are free to disregard them, since it claimed the solutions proposed in the document are ignorant of economic history.

Contrary to the editorial's view, the social encyclicals always involve moral teaching, though they do not claim to be infallible, and Catholics are free to debate and improve on these documents. But they are meant to be taken seriously, especially when the issues are of such crucial importance for the entire planet.

In 1891 Pope Leo XIII defended the struggle for a just wage that would support a family, and endorsed workers' rights to form unions and to strike. He called for a much wider distribution of wealth, along with state intervention to ensure just social conditions and regulation of the economy. These are basic moral issues that remain fundamental in all countries, not least in Australia.

Catholics are free to debate the details of how best to evaluate and implement these aspirations, but the matters are seriously commended to the consciences of Catholics with the full authority of the Church's social teaching. These are the principles of a 'fair go' that helped make Australia prosperous and reasonably equitable.

The same applies to the ideas in *Laudato Si'*. The issues have changed somewhat since Leo XIII's time, but they remain critical moral issues about the wellbeing of billions of people today. Francis considers these issues to be of the upmost urgency, and so is making this extraordinary appeal to all people, whatever their beliefs, to recognise that, on the advice of overwhelming scientific opinion, global warming is increasing dangerously, and the world needs urgently to

---

57. Ross Gittins, 'Banks Use Us to Hedge their Bets as they Speculate', *The Age*, 2 February 2016.

adjust not only our carbon emissions but also to use resources more equitably and sustainably.

Conclusion

While defenders of neoliberalism and its version of free markets often talk of the market in abstract terms, they not only have ignored the lessons of economic history themselves but even the economic carnage resulting from the Global Financial Crisis. Moreover, every other day reveals new scandals, not just in the predatory behaviour of vulture funds but even in leading companies like Volkswagen, General Motors, Johnson & Johnson and other pharmaceutical companies charging exorbitant prices beyond any financial justification. Australia's Commonwealth Bank has admitted to serious fraud and misconduct, and some are questioning the oligopolistic concentration of financial power in the Big Four Banks, which are valued at over $360 billion. They claimed assets in 2015 of some $3.5 trillion—about ten times the value of BHP and RIO combined—and posted profits of over thirty billion dollars. Because of the concentration of banking in Australia, the International Monetary Fund in 2012 warned about the risks they would face in another global financial crisis.[58]

Various commentators have blamed the populist and polarised political climate in the United States on the growing outrage among many Americans at the unfairness of their economic system, with the failure of the democratic processes to remedy the extreme and growing inequality. According to Desmond Lachman, a scholar at the conservative American Enterprise Institute no less, 'If unchecked, crony capitalism will continue to sap vitality out of the US economy and to undermine public support for the American model of capitalism.' John Kehoe commented that years of rent-seeking and manipulation of the economy to serve powerful vested interests are undermining US political stability. Alarm bells should be ringing about the dangers of 'crony capitalism'.[59]

---

58. Pat McConnell, 'Banking Outlook: Threats from Technology, Burst of Housing Bubble, End of Mining Boom', *The Conversation*, at <http://theconversation.com/profiles/pat-mcconnell-13137>. Accessed 14 March 2016.
59. John Kehoe, 'Regulation: Crony Capitalists are Killing Faith in the Markets', *The Australian Financial Review,* 4 January 2016.

As the eminent sociologist Amitai Etzioni wrote of the United States: 'Economic interest gained great power over the elected officials, who do not regulate the corporations that seem to lose any sense of self-restraint. We shall face such harm as long as capitalism, which works best when it is reined in, remains unbridled.'[60] This is true not just for the United States of course, but globally.

These are precisely the concerns of Pope Francis which are well supported by mainstream economists and commentators as we face unprecedented climate change and extreme social and economic inequalities. Francis warns that politics 'must not be subject to the economy' and highlights the 'urgent need for politics and economics to enter into a frank dialogue in the service of life, especially human life.' He laments that the financial crisis of 2007–8 'provided an opportunity to develop a new economy, more attentive to ethical principles, and new ways of regulating speculative financial practices and virtual wealth', but the response failed to rethink 'the outdated criteria which continue to rule the world.' (*LS* 189). He urges new creativity 'to promote a sustainable and equitable development within the context of a broader concept of quality of life.' (*LS* 192).

History will judge between the Pope and his critics in *The Australian* and elsewhere, as Francis endeavours to articulate a renewed moral perspective with which to build a fairer and more sustainable economy. The stakes are immensely high, and I suspect it is not Francis who will be judged extremely harshly.

---

60. Amitai Etzioni, 'Unbridled Capitalism: New Evidence', *Huffington Post*, at <http://www.huffingtonpost.com/amitai-etzioni/unbridled-capitalism-new_b_8177598.html?ir=Australia>. Accessed 23 September 2015.

Is Pope Francis Pro-life? Overcoming the Silence of *Laudato Si'* on Human Overpopulation

Peter MJ Hess

The question of human overpopulation is receiving increasingly serious attention from the scientific wing of the environmental movement. A generation ago authors such as Paul and Anne Ehrlich and Garrett Hardin sounded the warning about skyrocketing human numbers,[1] and James Kunstler addressed it *The Long Emergency.*[2] More recently, scientists Anthony Barnosky and Elizabeth Hadley ask how close we are to significant tipping points that might push us over the edge into climate and resource catastrophe.[3]

However, among theologians and ethicists—including those who demonstrate sensitivity to some ecological questions—there seems almost to be a conspiracy of silence surrounding the problem of overpopulation. Pope Francis echoes this silence in his encyclical *Laudato Si'* Senor (2015). On re-reading it a year after publication I find myself asking, 'Does Pope Francis really understand the issues? Is he really "pro-life"?' The pope had a fantastic opportunity—from the most visible pulpit in the world—to address the causes and treatments of one of the greatest present dangers to life on earth: anthropogenic climate change. I am glad he took this opportunity and I hope he'll revisit the topic.

---

1. Paul R Ehrlich and Anne E Ehrlich, *The Population Explosion* (New York: Simon and Schuster, 1990); Garrett Hardin, *Living Within Limits: Ecology, Economics, and Population Taboos* (Oxford, 1993).
2. James Kunstler, *The Long Emergency: Confronting the Converging Catastrophes of the Twenty-first Century* (2005).
3. Anthony Barnosky and Elizabeth Hadley, *Tipping Point for Planet Earth: How Close Are We to the Edge?* (Thomas Dunne Books, 2016).

But the encyclical leaves one glaring omission: not once in for-ty-thousand words did Pope Francis say a single thing about one of the two critical drivers of accelerating environmental degradation: human overpopulation. By our sheer numbers as well as our lifestyle, we *Homo sapiens* are driving huge numbers of our fellow species— and possibly our own as well—toward the precipice of extinction. In this respect the document's analysis and treatment of a complex problem is surprisingly weak.

Please do not mistake this as an anti-Catholic diatribe. I write as a lifelong Roman Catholic and a trained theologian. I have deep loyal-ty to my church and her gospel of freedom, to her ministries of heal-ing the sick, feeding the hungry, clothing the naked, and educating tens of millions around the world. I believe that how we live our faith in light of climate change may be the biggest ecclesiological issue of our time: without a livable world there will be no church at all.

There have been a few theological voices crying in the wilderness, such as Arthur McCormack who articulated a powerful case for the necessity of a religious response to the question in his incisive work *The Population Explosion: A Christian Concern.*[4] In the 1970s Daniel Callahan, Donald Lee, and Rita Hessley contributed to a brief schol-arly debate about the relative priority of freedom, justice, and secu-rity-survival as foundational values in their discussion of procreative ethics.[5] Important treatments in the 1990s included Susan Power Bratton's *Six Billion and More* and John Cobb's *Sustainability: Eco-nomics, Ecology and Justice.*[6] The Jesuit publication *America* afforded space in one issue for no fewer than three articles on the question. And the non-denominational *Ministry for Justice in Population Con-cerns* tried to ensure that discussions of population growth did not

---

4. Arthur McCormack, *The Population Explosion: A Christian Concern* (Harper Torchbooks, 1970).

5. Daniel Callahan, 'Ethics and Population Limitations: What Ethical Norms Should be Brought to Bear in Controlling Population Growth?', *Science,* 175 (1972): 487–94; Donald C Lee, 'Some Ethical Decision Criteria with Regard to Procreation', in *Environmental Ethics,* 1 (1979): 65–69; and Rita K Hessley, 'Should Government Regulate Procreation? A Third View', in *Environmental Ethics,* 3 (1981): 49–53.

6. Susan Power Bratton, *Six Billion and More: Human Population Regulation and Christian Ethics* (Louisville: Westminster/John Knox Press, 1992); John B Cobb, Jr, *Sustainability: Economics, Ecology and Justice* (New York: Maryknoll, 1992).

take place in abstraction from the urgent questions of social justice with which they are inextricably intertwined.[7]

Why should religious leaders and thinkers care about human overpopulation? For decades scientists have anxiously been watching the approaching intersection of two ominous curves: the ascending curve of net human population growth, and the descending curves of finite fossil fuels, fresh water, arable land, species diversity, and breathable air. With the net human population increasing by 250,000 persons per day, one million every four days, 90 million per year, these tangled intersection of these conflicting trends is already happening. Overpopulation and its attendant climate change has already caused famines, resource wars, spasms of genocide, and ecological refugeeism on a massive scale. Such trends will only get worse as the world gets hotter, climatologically less stable, and much more crowded by 2050. Religious leaders certainly should be concerned about this.

Pope Francis' letter *Laudato Si'* correctly identifies human-caused climate change as one of the greatest environmental threats facing the planet today. But the letter fell short of the mark if measured as an effective analysis of and response to the problems of global climate change. Along with global overconsumption of finite resources, overpopulation is one of the twin pillars underlying all our ecological crises. Together they account for the exhaustion in a few centuries of fossil fuels laid down over hundreds of millions of years. Together they are responsible for skyrocketing CO_2, melting glaciers and rising sea levels, inundation of island nations and coastal cities, and accelerating ecological refugeeism around the globe. Together they account for coral reef bleaching, deforestation, habitat destruction, and worldwide extinction of species on a scale unseen for millions of years.

In a century and a half the human population skyrocketed from one billion to 7.42 billion, fueled by a one-time bonanza of fossil energy. The industrial application of fossil fuels improved agriculture and furthered the advance of science and technology. More food meant fewer people died of starvation, and modern medicine found ways to decrease the death rate and increase the human life span.

---

7.   Based in Los Angeles, the now-defunct MJPC included as affiliated members the
     Unitarian Church, the United Church of Christ, the Evangelical Lutheran Synod,
     and other denominations.

So why does a 'pro-life' pope fail to recognize that human overpopulation is a problem for all life on earth? Of the sixteen occurrences of the word 'population' in *Laudato Si'*, only three are relevant. These are found in paragraph 50, in the context of the discussion of human numbers. The first instance is a flat-out denial: 'while it is true that an unequal distribution of the population and of available resources creates obstacles to development and to a sustainable use of the environment, it must nonetheless be recognized that demographic growth is fully compatible with an integral and shared development'. Pope Francis seems unable or unwilling to acknowledge that there is a biological limit to Earth's carrying capacity for humans just as there is for every other species on the planet.

The second use of the term correctly points to the arrogance and danger of ignoring excessive consumption: 'To blame population growth instead of extreme and selective consumerism on the part of some, is one way of refusing to face the issues.' Indeed, it would be completely wrong to point fingers elsewhere and ignore the thirty-times-greater environmental impact of children born in the developed world over those born in developing nations: 'It is an attempt to legitimize the present model of distribution, where a minority believes that it has the right to consume in a way which can never be universalized.' The pope correctly addresses here the second pillar of environmental degradation.

But the pope's third reference shows that his understanding of population issues does not reflect the fact of biological equilibrium: 'Attention needs to be paid to imbalances in population density, on both national and global levels, since a rise in consumption would lead to complex regional situations.' The claim that population density is a merely local problem can be shown to be false on many counts. The delicate balance between earth's inhabitants is constrained by numerous factors related to the population of competing species.

Let us look at just one of many indicators of the impact of human numbers—the decline of 'charismatic megafauna'. Lions once ranged widely across Africa and into Syria, Israel, Iraq, Pakistan, Iran, and northwest India. 2,000 years ago more than a million lions roamed the Earth; today there may be as few as 20,000 left. Demographers estimate the African human population will be four billion by 2100, equivalent to the entire global population in 1974. The causes of lion decline are directly related to human population growth: loss of habitat, replacement of prey species by livestock, retaliatory killings, trophy hunting, consumption of lion meat, commercial sale of body parts, and introduced disease.

Tigers likewise are in precipitous decline: the Bengal Tiger population stood at 100,000 in 1900, and numbered fewer than 4,000 in in 2013. With India at 1.4 billion humans today, the human/tiger ratio is 35,000 to one. Examples of other fauna being crowded out by humans include African elephants, rhinoceros, pandas, polar bears, sharks, whales, and other large species.[8]

By our sheer numbers we humans are presiding over the sixth great mass extinction event in the history of earth, and ultimately we are as vulnerable as the other species we are extinguishing. We may temporarily have removed some of our natural constraints, but eventually our excess population beyond carrying capacity will be pitilessly trimmed by the factors of famine, disease, refugeeism, and brutal wars over water, energy, land, and resources. This eventuality should be recognized as a serious moral problem for a pro-life position. Twenty-five years ago Catholic missionary Sean McDonagh asked, 'Is it really pro-life to ignore the warnings of demographers and ecologists who predict that unbridled population growth will lead to severe hardship and an increase in the infant mortality rate for succeeding generations? Is it pro-life to allow the extinction of hundreds of thousands of living species which will ultimately affect the well-being of all future generations on the planet?'[9]

Pope Francis has said many important things in *Laudato Si'*, and my critique should not detract from what is an excellent first foray by Catholic Church leadership into discussions of ecological degradation. But sweeping overpopulation under the carpet is like leaving the eggs out of eggs Benedict. I hope *Laudato Si'* is only the first installment in a courageous reappraisal of theology-as-status-quo, and that we can look forward soon to another encyclical addressing the problem of human overpopulation in its relationship with overconsumption.

The encyclical launches an odd attack on air conditioning:
People may well have a growing ecological sensitivity but it has not succeeded in changing their harmful habits of consumption which,

---

8. See http://fpesa.net/fpesa-research-paper-assessment-human-population-growth-threatens-animal-species/
9. Sean McDonagh, *The Greening of the Church* (New York: Maryknoll, 1990), 65.

rather than de- creasing, appear to be growing all the more. A simple example is the increasing use and power of air-conditioning. The markets, which immediately benefit from sales, stimulate ever greater demand. An outsider looking at our world would be amazed at such behavior, which at times appears self-destructive (55).

Perhaps the papal apartments in Castelgondolfo do not need air conditioning, but in many hotter parts of the world, both desert and tropical, air conditioning can be life-saving for hundreds of millions in hotter parts of the world.

However, there is greater dilatoriness on the part of some denominations than others, and some among theologians and philosophers a tacit avoidance of the topic still prevails. As a Roman Catholic, I am particularly disturbed that my own church leaders have consistently demonstrated remarkably little concern about population matters, or have at best glossed over their more crucial dimensions. Pope John Paul II's 1989 encyclical message on *The Ecological Crisis: A Common Responsibility* is profoundly silent on the question. Despite the many fine things the Pope has to say about environmental degradation as a moral problem, and about the necessity of justice and solidarity between rich and poor nations in the quest for solutions, he does not even mention failure to restrain the exercise of our procreative capacities among the elements enumerated as lying at the root of ecological breakdown. The two brief paragraphs devoted to the demographic question in his *Sollicitudo Rei Socialis* emphasise only the pope's alarm over governments 'launching systematic campaigns against birth', and his concern over the drop in birthrate in the northern hemisphere which might prejudice its further economic development.[10]

A few shafts of light indicate that even in Catholicism the theological window may be slowly opening on the question of over-population. The American Catholic Bishops' 1991 pastoral letter on the environment, *Renewing the Earth*, includes a brief discussion of the issue, although regrettably the authors quickly rebar the shutters by minimising the seriousness of human numbers in comparison with the more popularly palatable issue of human over-consumption, which they identify as 'the greatest single source of global environ-

---

10. Pope John Paul II, *Sollicitudo Rei Socialis (On Social Concern)* (Washington, DC: U.S. Catholic Conference, 1987), 42.

mental destruction.[11] In contrast, a recent editorial in the *National Catholic Reporter* was much more frank in its assessment of the grim implications of the Worldwatch Institute's 1994 *State of the World Report*, suggesting that on the question of population our church 'needs to get its hands dirty by dealing with the world as it is and not solely as it should be'.[12] And Edward Echlin has recently suggested in the English periodical *The Month* that Catholic theology's acknowledgment of population control as a necessity might have implications for the human community as revolutionary as the discovery of fire.[13]

Understanding the Conspiracy of Silence

The reasons for assuming an ostrich-like position on the question of population are legion. Some are private—such as the simple desire to have a large family—a desire that necessarily tends to preclude the conscious recognition of the problematic nature of unrestricted procreation. Or one might feel uncomfortable discussing a question that appears to cast blame on those with traditionally large families. In response I can only suggest that although discussion need not be avoided for these reasons, it must be conducted in as neutral and non-judgmental a fashion as possible. For the many theologians and ethicists who do not share a personal interest in unlimited procreation, the reasons inhibiting discussion of over-population are reducible to eight broad categories.

vincible ignorance

The first is 'vincible ignorance about biological facts'. Many have never considered why it is impossible for a finite planet to support an infinitely expanding human population, and why the hope of exporting our surplus people to other planets must remain in the realm of pure fantasy.[14] Faith in the reliability of the established order is so strong that we seldom attempt to imagine future terrestrial condi-

---

11. The United States Conference of Catholic Bishops, 'Renewing the Earth: An Invitation to Reflection and Action on the Environment in Light of Catholic Social Teaching by the US Bishops', in *Origins*, 21 (1991): 430.
12. *National Catholic Reporter*, 30/13 (28 January, 1994).
13. Edward P Echlin, 'Population and Catholic Theology: Discovering Fire Anew', in *The Month* (January, 1992): 38.
14. Garrett Hardin, *Living within Limits*, 9–13.

tions beyond two or three generations. We simply assume that the panda, the rhino, the snow leopard, and the California Condor will always be with us, just as our forbears no doubt assumed that bison were inexhaustible and that the Grizzly bear would always roam California.

Furthermore, scholars often carry the presuppositional liabilities that come with living in an urban context. When our immediate environment of housing tracts and shopping malls does not change perceptibly from day to day, it takes an act of imagination to recognize that milk comes not from cartons but from dairy herds whose fields are being inexorably paved over, that water flowing from our faucets has a finite provenance in the Nile River or the Ogalala aquifer, and that the heat emanating from our radiators is generated by our one-time bonanza of fossil fuels.[15] Vincible ignorance can be overcome by educating people to the vast and growing body of reliable sources on sustainability and the multi-faceted ecological crisis, such as the Worldwatch Institute's annual *State of the World* reports.

invincible ignorance

A more obstinate position might be termed 'invincible ignorance', a theological commitment to the idea that God in the exercise of divine providence would never allow a population problem to exist. At a conference of the *North American Conference on Christianity and Ecology*, I assisted in organizing a panel discussion on the moral dimensions of human over-population, in which the factors of gender and denomination seemed to influence the panelists' positions. Only the (female) Protestant pastor forthrightly declared that human numbers definitely constitute a problem, and that it is morally incumbent upon us at this time to rectify it. The (male) Catholic priest asserted that though we do not yet face a population crunch, it is conceivable that there might come a time when we would find it morally obligatory to limit the number of children we bring into the world. The (male) Orthodox priest insisted that there could never be a population problem, as that would negate God's creative power and providence.[16]

---

15. Anne and Paul Ehlich, *The Population Explosion*, chapter 2.
16. San Francisco, 1991. The Bay Area chapter of Zero Population Growth declined to participate.

apocalyptic language

A third reason for reluctance to discuss the question is that the case for over-population is often presented in excessively alarmist or even repellent language. Christopher Derrick has rightly noted that population control advocates often employ gratuitously apocalyptic language, such as declaring that without restrictive measures the very survival of the planet is at stake. He cites for example Paul Ehrlich's over-statement in *The Population Bomb* that 'current rates of population growth guarantee an environmental crisis which will persist until the final collapse'.[17] Even more deplorable is the reference by radical environmentalists to population as 'a plague',[18] or to human beings as a 'cancer' without which the earth would be far better off. We need more temperate language and an increased specificity in the use of terms. For example, although human *actions* may appear strongly analogous to the ultimate self-destructiveness of cancer, humanity *itself* cannot reasonably be compared with it, for in fact, quite the opposite is true: our hope for the solution of ecological problems can only lie in our rational human understanding and embrace of ecosystemic principles. And when we speak about human numbers as a threat to 'survival', we need to be more specific as to whether by that we mean the survival of the planet, or of the biosphere, or of higher mammals, or of the human species, or of technologically affluent society. Failure to so specify can only damage the credibility of our statements on population.

divergent estimates of carrying capacity

A fourth reason for dismissing the relevance of examining reproductive responsibility is that there is so much disagreement about how to define the meaning of 'over-population'. There are two dimensions to this disagreement, a cultural and a scientific dimension. In a multi-cultural world the delicate question 'what is over-population?' is not easily answered in terms of mere numbers. An inhabitant of Wyoming comfortable with 4.8 persons per square mile might find

---

17. Christopher Derrick, *Too Many People? A Problem in Values* (San Francisco: Ignatius Press, 1985), 10–13, citing page 47 of *The Population Bomb* (1975).
18. Kingsley Davis, 'The Climax of Population Growth,' *California Medicine*, 113 (1970): 33–39. Cited in Jacqueline Kasun, *The War Against Population* (San Francisco: Ignatius Press, 1988), 32.

teeming Manhattan intolerably claustrophobic, just as a resident of Hong Kong accustomed to 14,542 residents per square mile might find rural China's 327 people per square mile hopelessly empty.[19]

However, from a scientific perspective density is not the only relevant issue.[20] The scientific dimension of our problem involves biological absolutes, which can be expressed in terms of carrying capacity, 'the maximum population of a given animal or of humans that an ecosystem can support without being degraded or destroyed in the long run'.[21] Estimates of global human carrying capacity vary widely enough that to the cynic they might appear non-sensical. *People for Open Space* estimated (1994) that the long-term carrying capacity of the Earth is one billion persons, or 50 million on a hunter-gatherer basis if we desire to safeguard all other species from extinction. The Ehrlichs calculate that in terms of sustainable humanly-manipulated biomass, approximately two billion humans might be supported indefinitely by the Earth.[22] *Friends of the Earth* reckoned that without our use of nitrate-based fertilizer (dependent on finite fossil fuels), the number is somewhere between one and three billion.[23] The organisation Negative Population Growth would like to see global humanity reduced to about two billion.[24]

These figures are all admittedly unnerving to us who have gotten used to a human world that has silently grown to 7.42 billion-double the most optimistic of the estimates-without any apparent problems so far in feeding most of the population most of the time. But the are hardly more unbelievable than the extravagant views of cornucopian economist Julian Simon, who confidently proclaimed that there are no identifiable theoretical limits to the number of people that the earth's resources can support.[25] The world greets one million new human inhabitants every four days, for a net increase of ninety-five

19. All figures are drawn from the publication *Statistical Abstract of the United States* (Washington DC: United States Department of Commerce, 1993), Chart 1374.
20. See for example the discussion of the non-self-sustaining character of the Netherlands' dense population, in Ehrlich, *The Population Explosion*, 38.
21. Bernard J Nebel, *Environmental Science: The Way the World Works*, third edition (Prentice-Hall, 1981), 573.
22. Paul and Anne Ehrlich, *The Population Explosion*, 1990.
23. All three estimates were acquired during telephone interviews with the people or organizations in question, in the summer of 1988.
24. Newsletter of Negative Population Growth, 1993.
25. Julian Simon, *The Ultimate Resource* (Princeton, 1981), 42–52.

million per year, and many demographers agree that the global population will reach ten billion before it stabilizes at replacement rate in the twenty-first century.

World-wide food production capacity is only one determiner of carrying capacity. Others include sufficient energy to fuel indefinitely our consumer-oriented culture, adequate land for habitation and agriculture, and permanently adequate water supplies that do not depend upon the finite capital of gradually sinking aquifers collected through eons of slow percolation.

Furthermore, unless we assume that only humans count, it would appear that our execution of the anthropocene extinction event—through the pressure of an ever-expanding human population—is itself a moral evil. In *Too Many People? A Problem in Values*, Christopher Derrick rejects consideration of the rights of any sentient beings other than human.[26] Taken in one sense, his teleological assumption that 'people are for God' is reflective of the best in Christian anthropology. However, his use of it to underpin the categorical denial that there could ever be 'too many people' is coupled with an absence of discussion of the other elements of the biosphere. In fact, Derrick completely ignores ecosystemic questions, interpreting the population problem largely in terms of world hunger, and declaring that the only problem is one of inequitable distribution rather than one of the chronic insufficient production of food. Yet we must ask ourselves whether if it lies within our power as a species to stop unraveling the web of life by controlling our own reproduction, we have an obligation to preach and teach and work by example toward that goal. The security of our fellow living creatures is a moral factor often overlooked by those who interpret carrying capacity primarily in terms of whether we can produce sufficient bread for the world.

thralldom to economic growth

Many theologians and ethicists who properly concern themselves with issues of social justice in world economic development have consciously or unconsciously adopted the standard assumption of economists that growth is necessarily good in and of itself. Without continual growth in consumption and population, stagnation will re-

---

26. Christopher Derrick, *Too Many People? A Problem in Values* (San Francisco: Ignatius Press, 1985), chap. 5.

sult and people will suffer.[27] The foresightful work of the few scholars such as Herman Daly and John Cobb who have written on steady-state economics remains decidedly removed from the mainstream,[28] which persists in the belief that there are no theoretical limits on resource availability. Moreover, there appears to be a clear commonality of assumptions between proponents of this dominant economic paradigm and the ideological opponents of population control. Jacqueline Kasun devoted most of her book *The War Against Population* to a history and critique of the population control movement, but spent one brief chapter demolishing what she regarded as the gloomy 'lifeboat economics' of 'doomsayers' such as the authors of the *Global 2000* report. She seconding the rosy prognostications of Roger Revelle and of Colin Clarke, who believed respectively that the earth could indefinitely support 40 billion or 100 billion people.[29] That such optimistic figures are accepted as credible by theologians is exemplified in David Toolan's editorial in *America Magazine* that 'some experts estimate that if the third world used modern methods of agriculture, it would be capable of sustaining a population of 30 billion'.[30]

In response to this assumption about the virtually limitless capacity of the earth and its resources, I suggest that most scientists have a much firmer understanding of the facts regarding human ecological dependence than do most economists, who often regard issues of pollution and resource depletion as an externality of only peripheral significance. For the biologist, maintaining the stability of the ecosystem upon which we all depend cannot in the long run be regarded as

27. A fine example of the elaboration of this assumption may be found in James A Weber's *Grow or Die!* (New Rochelle, NY: Arlington House, 1970).

28. Herman E Daly and John B Cobb, *For the Common Good: Redirecting the Economy toward Community, the Environment, and a Sustainable Future* (Boston: Beacon Press, 1989). See also other works by Daly, such as *Steady-State Economics: The Economics of Biophysical Equilibrium and Moral Growth* (San Francisco: WH Freeman, 1977), and *Economics, Ecology, Ethics: Essays Toward a Steady State Economy* (San Francisco: WH Freeman, 1980); and of William Ophuls, *Economics and the Politics of Scarcity: A Prologue to a Political Theory of the Steady State* (San Francisco: WH Freeman, 1977).

29. Jacqueline Kasun, *The War against Population: The Economics and Ideology of Population Control* (San Francisco: Ignatius Press, 1988), 34–35.

30. David S Toolan, 'Second Thoughts about the Population Bomb', in *America*, 168 (1993): 16.

an economic externality. Rather, it must be acknowledged as vital to the health of human society, to the survival of our fellow species, and even to the continued theorizing of economists. In fact, it is human technological culture which in the long perspective might be regarded as an externality. The question of population growth will only be treated effectively when we have integrated our assumptions about human economic activity with our understanding of the broader economy of nature.

causal over-simplification

Some population control advocates fail to state the case in a sensitive and balanced way that takes into account the enormous range of issues involved. Often ignored is the fundamental interrelationship of ecological sustainability and economic justice. Our crisis is not just about how many of us there are, but about how we live, and in particular about how well a few of us live in comparison to the rest of us. By now it is a cliché to reckon that a child born in the industrially urbanized United States may exert a lifetime environmental impact—in the form of resource and energy consumption and in waste production—that is thirty times greater than that of a child born in rural Africa or India. A sophisticated approach to the population problem must obviously involve far more than the simplistic and patronizing judgment that poorer nations must stop having so many babies before they can receive developmental assistance.

Garrett Hardin's landmark essay 'Lifeboat Ethics: the Case against Helping the Poor', revealed two significant shortcomings. First, Hardin made the tendentious insinuation that the rendering of developmental assistance and direct unconditional food aid is a naive and kind-hearted "liberal" approach in contrast to a sensible conservative realism. The more serious flaw was his setting up a straw-man argument—in the form of a crude and easily demolished definition of justice as equality—concluding that justice is simply not applicable in the world of foreign hardball politics.[31]

It will be unfortunate if discussion of human over-population continued to be side-tracked by self-serving arguments by inhabitants of developed countries. Hardin was right about global sustainability

---

31. Garrett Hardin, 'Lifeboat Ethics: the Case against Helping the Poor', in *Psychology Today* (August, 1974): 38–43, 123–26.

and the tragedy of the commons, but his arguments need to be articulated in a more sophisticated way than metaphors about lifeboats will allow, at least when our lifeboats are being constructed from resources commandeered from developing countries in the form of crushing interest payments on foreign debt.

It is imperative that environmentalists adopt a more integrated approach to the population question, perhaps along the lines of the "I=PxAxT" equation developed by Anne and Paul Ehrlich in *The Population Explosion*. The Ehrlichs suggest that the most fruitful way to measure the human impact on the environment is to express it as a function of three general kinds of variable: the total population of a given culture, multiplied by its level of affluence, multiplied by the nature of its technology.[32] Our moral analysis of population growth must involve judgments about the fundamental restructuring of social, political, and economic systems, commencing with those of the developed nations. Human justice is a precondition of ecological sustainability, and the pursuit of justice will necessitate the acquiescence of the privileged few to substantial and even drastic reductions in our material standard of living, without which we have no right to expect others to take seriously our call for a reduction in worldwide birthrate. In Rita Hessley's careful articulation of the question, justice is the paramount value without which neither the freedom of the individual nor the survival of the species is meaningful.[33]

vested theological and moral interests

Over-population inevitably impinges upon highly sensitive areas in the ethical and moral theological discussion of human life, such as the acceptability of abortion or artificial contraception. This need not be an insurmountable obstacle, however, for it is certainly possible to discuss demographic questions while respecting the requirements of contrasting moral theologies. The Roman Catholic Church will not accept abortion as a convenient solution, for abortion is certainly as much a sin against creation as is the failure to protect endangered species.[34] On the other hand, many Catholic moral theologians no

---

32. *The Population Explosion*, 58-59.
33. Rita K Hessley, 'Should Government Regulate Procreation? A Third View', in *Environmental Ethics*, 3 (1981): 51–52.
34. *Renewing the Earth*, 430.

longer accept a summary condemnation of so-called 'artificial' contraception, and the conventional distinction itself between what is
natural and what is unnatural is no longer entirely convincing. Edward Echlin notes that 'because married people are within nature,
with unique responsibility for the rest of nature, may we not go so
far as to say that failure to control biological processes which could
unsustainably exploit nature is unnatural?'[35]

The issue of contraception is in any case logically separable from
the question of whether or not people *ought* to limit the number of
their children. For even if in the practical order of things a workable
population limitation program will almost certainly have to include
the widespread conscientious use of so-called 'artificial' methods of
contraception, the questions of responsible family planning and of
whether or not there exists a basic human right to unlimited procreation can be discussed in abstraction from debates about the morality of means by which conception may be controlled.

A valuable approach is to locate the debate about human numbers
in a wider moral theological context that emphasizes the sanctity of
all life on earth. Years of Catholic missionary experience in the Phil-
ippines gave Sean McDonagh an intimate knowledge of the causes
and consequences of environmental degradation, prompting him to
place discussion of the sanctity of human life firmly within an ecological context:

> Is it really pro-life to ignore the warnings of demographers and ecolo-
> gists who predict that unbridled population growth will lead to severe
> hardship and an increase in the infant mortality rate for succeeding
> generations? Is it pro-life to allow the extinction of hundreds of thou-
> sands of living species which will ultimately affect the well-being of all
> future generations on the planet?[36]

Thus there are at least two responses to the fear that acknowledging
human over-population opens a Pandora's box for moral theology.
First, it is possible to discuss the issue in a manner that respects dif-
fering moral opinions on problematic questions. Even though the
hierarchical church clearly shows no signs of reversing its stand on

---

35. Population and Catholic Theology: Discovering Fire Anew," 36.
36. Sean McDonagh, *The Greening of the Church* (New York: Maryknoll, 1990),
    65.

artificial contraception,[37] it is both feasible and urgently necessary to include the necessity of limiting family size in environmental ethical discussions. Second, and more importantly, the population issue is not going to disappear, and failure to act courageously now in including reverence for all life in our discussions of both the environment and of human reproductive morality will only postpone the inevitable judgments that will have to be made about what constitutes reverence for life in a crowded world, and about which lives merit it most.

fear of coercion

A final motivation to sweep the population question under the environmental rug is fear that any admission of risk in perpetual expansion of the human community might lead to the attempted justification of coercive measures, such as involuntary abortion or sterilization. The threat of coercion is certainly of concern to us all and particularly to women, who have as much reason to reject being told what children they may not have as what children they must have. The use of financial pressure or physical force to limit family size could be ruled out, and a number of intelligent and careful ethical analyses of coercive measures have been made, for example by Daniel Callahan and Susan Power Bratton.[38]

While the freedom to procreate lies on an ontologically different plane from my freedom to smoke, a comparison is useful. The two actions share in the quality of being instances of private behavior which carry significant social consequences. If I may rightfully be prevented from smoking in a crowded elevator to protect others from the danger of second-hand smoke, why may not I be legitimately prevented from imposing increased environmental risks upon our collective grandchildren by my procreating without limit?

---

37. Pope John Paul II, *Veritatis Splendor: The Splendor of the Truth Regarding Certain Fundamental questions of the Church's Moral Teaching* (Encyclical Letter, August 6, 1993), sect. 80–83.
38. Daniel Callahan, 'Ethics and Population Limitation', in *Ethics and Population*, edited by Michael D Bayles (Cambridge, Mass: Schenkman Publishing Co, 1976), chapter 2, 19–40; Susan Power Bratton, *Six Billion and More*, chapter 5, 'Coercion and Abortion in Population Management', 175–201.

Of course, coercion must used as only a last resort, and would therefore only be justifiable if both (a) all voluntary measures to halt population growth have failed, and (b) human numbers have reached a level that threatens the survival of the community. The determination of when all voluntary methods had been exhausted is a matter for extreme care. Likewise, 'survival' is a term whose meaning would have to be precisely defined: do we intend by this the survival of our species alone, or of our affluent techno-logical society, or of other species, or of the biosphere in all its complexity?

Moral suasion in the form of comprehensive ecological education programs is eminently more acceptable, being more consonant with reason and human dignity. Discussion of the danger of over-popu-lation must be conducted in such a way as to respect persons and cherish individual rights to self-determination. However, the rights of individuals can ultimately be ensured only in a context that also secures the common good by including future human generations within the community and by respecting the integrity of global eco-systems. Failure now to take the demographic bull by the horns only renders it more likely that the reproductive rights of some future generation will be gored by coercive policies.

Conclusions

In conclusion, in the words of one member of the radical environ-mental movement, unless we take prompt steps to tackle the popula-tion question, in the words of Dave Foreman of *Earth First!*, all of our other well-intentioned efforts will be comparable only to rearranging the deck chairs on the *Titanic*. If we have an obligation to ensure that our descendants inhabit an earth reflective of the primal beauty of creation, then surely it is incumbent upon Christian ecologists to take very seriously the question of human numbers. Pope John Paul II has declared that 'if a nation were to succumb more or less delib-erately to the temptation to close in upon itself and failed to meet the responsibilities following from its superior position in the com-munity of nations, it would fall seriously short of its ethical duty'.[39] I submit that on the basis of the increasingly clear evidence from fields

---

39. *Sollicitudo Rei Socialis*, 23.

as diverse as agronomy, climatology, and wildlife biology, the present and future impact of a steadily increasing human population on a limited planet cannot but be ecosystemically destructive. If as moral educators we refrain from speaking out on the matter of over-population, or worse yet, if we stifle legitimate discussion of these issues, are we not failing in our duty as ministers of the truth?

Integral Ecology, *Sister Death* and *Laudato Si'*[1]

Anthony J Kelly CSsR

Pope Francis has no romantic view of the world, given his robust denunciation of consumerism, his sensitivity to the sufferings of the earth and its people, his lamentation over the disappearance of so many species of fauna and flora, and his special reference to the deaths of the poor and infants [20, 20, 48].[2] All these are evidences of a sober realism. Nonetheless, there is little mention of death in *Laudato Si': On the Care for Our Common Home*. Nor does he include in his citation of the *Canticle of St Francis* the verse the saint added as his own death approached, 'Be praised my Lord through our Sister, Bodily Death, from whose embrace no living person can escape'. In the interests of a genuine integral ecology, therefore, this article considers the ecological and theological significance of death and how it affects and inspires 'care for our common home'.

Before moving to a consideration of 'Sister Death', a familiar presence in the life of this planet, we will pause over what we mean by an 'integral ecology', above all in *Laudato Si'*.[3] Negatively, an integral ecology is opposed to the two extremes, either that of reducing ecological methods to purely empirical procedures and technocratic controls; or to, say, a green spirituality that disdains the findings of

---

1. Previously published in *Laudato Si': An Integral Ecology and the Catholic Vision* (Adelaide: ATF Press, 2016).

2. Numbers in square brackets correspond to the numbered paragraphs in *Laudato Si'*.

3. There are many references to 'integral' describing development, education and ecology in *Laudato Si'*, see especially paragraphs 10, 11, 62, 124, the whole of Chapter 4, 137, 141, 147, 159, 197, 225, 230. The phrase, 'integral ecology' first appears in a 2009 document of the International Theological Commission which recognises the need for the Catholic "natural law" tradition to be open to ecological perspectives—and for these to recognise a fundamental natural law. See, 'In search of universal ethic: A New Look at Natural Law', 82.

science. More positively, an integral outlook will presume an appreciation of the planetary environment, and show a capacity to diagnose how it has been harmed by uncaring exploitation. But this must be correlated to the 'inner ecology' of culture. Without a conversion of mind and heart, in both a personal and social sense, there can be little hope for any turnaround in our relationship to the world of nature and the delicate interrelationships and synergies it discloses. Further, without a shareable discourse on basic human values, the prospects of considering the common good or the integrity of the environment diminish. An integral ecology, therefore, must insist on the fact and mystery of death in the interdisciplinary collaborative framework it envisages. That will mean leaving unanswered questions that cannot be answered, and deferring to hope in Christ crucified and risen for a deeper appreciation of 'Sister Death' in the universe of God's creation.[4]

As this article progresses and examines various sensibilities and theoretical understandings regarding death, certain questions keep recurring as each position is outlined, such as how does this particular approach to death affect an integral ecology of our planetary environment and its responsibility for 'our common home'. By reflecting on death in an ecological context, we can ensure that the framework of integral ecology will remain open, and radically undecided, unless the witness of Christian faith and hope is invoked. In this way, faith in Christ is an ever renewable resource in a world of dwindling resources.

But that is to run ahead when efforts to name the reality of death tend to oscillate between two classic statements. The first expresses an immemorial sense of the tragedy of death: *sunt lacrimae rerum et mentem mortalia tangunt*[5] (translatable as, 'there are tears from human happenings and mortal sufferings touch the heart'). Such words can only intensify the widespread lament over the environmental destruction that has been wrought on the life of the planet, so often by human agencies. The other is the statement of the Johannine Jesus: 'Unless the grain of wheat falls into the earth and dies, it remains just a single grain; but if it dies, it bears much fruit' (Jn 12: 24). Here, too, there is an inevitable sense of diminishment, but it is taken up into

---

4. For an informed and inspiring account, see Denis Edwards, *Ecology at the Heart of Faith* (Maryknoll, NY: Orbis, 2006).

5. Virgil, *Aeneid*, I, 462.

the ultimate hope for transformation and communion. The implication is that death and dying have an essential place in life and serve the purposes of the 'sublime communion' [89] that God is bringing about. Admittedly, the fact and reality of death permit no theoretical synthesis of the psychological, philosophical, theological and ecological actors involved.[6] Nonetheless, the five headings under which this article will be presented, will, we hope, serve to deepen reflection and sharpen conscience.

1. The Deadliness of Death
2. The Denial of Death
3. Death in Christ
4. Before the Foundation of the World
5. The Realm of Otherness

The Deadliness of Death

While Paul declares that 'living is Christ, and dying is gain' (Phil 1:21), his words describe the hope of one who have arrived at the summit of Christian faith. On the other hand, the brute fact of death is a universal and intrusive reality, especially when it occurs in its most violent and alien form. Death figures in our cultural perceptions in two major ways. First, there is what might be regarded as a 'cooler' view. Death is a matter-of-fact biological reality. Indeed, it is a necessary feature inscribed in the dynamics of evolution. There can be no progress in the evolutionary scheme of things unless death ensures the succession of generations. It is the price to be paid for the evolution of life on earth. It makes possible the emergence of differentiated, complex living beings in a world of wonderful biodiversity. Unless we belonged to the mortal world of life on this planet, human beings would never have come into existence.[7]

---

6. Lucy Bregman, *Death, Dying, Spirituality and Religions. A Study of the Death Awareness Movement* (New York: Peter Lang, 2003) presents a many-faceted movement approaching the phenomenon of death as a meaningful experience beyond the specifically medical context. Her interdisciplinary movement can appear to be purely secular, but, in fact, it tends to draw on the spirituality latent in classic and popular expressions of Judaism, Christianity and Buddhism—and more besides.

7. Denis Edwards, *Breath of Life. A Theology of the Creator Spirit* (Maryknoll, NY: Orbis, 2004), 137-38; 174.

Moreover, there is a sober, scientific backdrop to individual death. It is the eventual collapse of the solar system, even if billions of years from now. And that will entail the extinction of all life on this planet. Of more dramatic menace is the most probable reoccurrence of cosmic events that have been lethal to planetary life in the past. William R Stoeger SJ, in his scientific account of catastrophes in this life-bearing universe, considers matters within a time-frame of 50 million years – enough time for the appearance and disappearance of a species. He writes,

> The prime reason for discussing [such possibilities] . . . is though they are remote and of long-time-scale occurrence, they are certain to happen. They also represent the ultimate demise of life on this planet, and, in the case of the universe, of the cosmic life-bearing womb itself. As such, they represent a very formidable challenge to our religious understanding of what ultimate destiny, eternal life, the resurrection of the body, and the new heavens and the new earth might mean.[8]

In other words, 'the mystery of life and death are written into the very heart and essence of material creation'.[9] The law of entropy is built into the cosmos itself. All systems break down; and the fundamental chaos which they order and control finally takes over. This point of view is characterised by a dispassionate scientific objectivity. An integral ecology is made to include a range of scientific data on the inevitable death of the universe. On the other hand, this outlook serves to highlight the wonder of life and all the varied lifeforms that have appeared in their improbable contingency. To this degree, *data* begin to appear as *dona*, and call forth gratitude to a giver for the gift of sheer existence.

There is a 'hot' version of death as well. The earth has lived under the threat of megadeath for decades. Though human history has always known its catalogue of natural disasters; famines, earthquakes, plagues. 'acts of God', we now live with the eerie possibility of death-dealing human activities affecting the planet. Biological warfare, thermonuclear incineration, and ecological destruction still

---

8. William R Stoeger,SJ, 'Scientific Accounts of Ultimate Catastrophes in our Life-Bearing Universe', in *The End of the World and the Ends of God*, edited by Polkinghorne and Welker (19–28), 21.

9. Stoeger, 'Scientific Accounts . . ', 28.

menace life on this planet. Huge technological systems shape the ecological, social, political and economic world. The consumerist economy is insatiable in its demands. Enormous military arsenals at the disposition of dozens of governments openly include weapons of mass destruction designed for biological or thermonuclear warfare. This range of lethal capacities is the material expression of a readiness to wipe out whole populations if the necessity arises. Given that the possibilities of 'heat death' are taken for granted in the contemporary environment, the task of an integral ecology is clarified, namely, to mitigate the probabilities of global self-destruction, so as to work for the disarmament of the heart, and the kind of reconciliation that can remove environmental threats from our common home.

The Denial of Death

After noting factual approaches to the inevitability of death, we now move on to more subjective considerations associated with the denial of such a reality.

The dread of death goes some way in explaining morbid aspects of modern culture, such as: obsessive consumerism, deracinated individualism and careless destruction of the environment. As Ernest Becker expresses the thesis of his now classic work, *The Denial of Death*:

> The idea of death, the fear of it, haunts the human animal like nothing else; it is the mainspring of human activity—activity designed largely to avoid the fatality of death, to overcome it by denying in some way that it is the final destiny for man.[10]

Though Becker acknowledges the enormous influence of Freud in the understanding of psychopathology, he is also critical. For Becker, the fundamental repression or denial in human life is not related to the sexual, as Freud had taught, but to death. Hence, the purpose of therapy is to free the suffering person to live with the most radical fear of all, which has its origin in our common mortality. But what, then, are human beings to do with the fact that they and the natural world they inhabit are all inevitably on the way to death?

Melancholic though such a question might sound, it poses deeper questions about urgent ecological matters and their larger cos-

---

10. Ernest Becker, *The Denial of Death* (New York: The Free Press, 1973), ix.

mic connections. Becker insists that we face the primordial terror that affects the human psyche in the face of death, and this means a radical acceptance of creaturehood. As creatures, we are immersed in the wholeness of nature, connected to it, caught up and carried along by it. The paradox is that only by accepting our limitation and contingency within a larger whole, only by yielding ourselves up to the life-process, this stream of life and death, can we arrive at true freedom and psychic health.

Religious experience, Becker argues, is essentially a 'creature feeling' in the face of the massive transcendence of creation. In this respect, the human is a tiny, vulnerable instance of existence within the overwhelming miracle of the universe. At this juncture, 'religion and psychology find a talking point right at the point of the problem of courage'.[11] Faced with the immensity of the universe and its apparent impassivity in regard to individual fate,

> man had to invent and create out of himself the limitations of perception and equanimity to live on this planet. And so the core of psychodynamics, the formation of the human character, is a study in human self-limitation and in the terrifying costs of that limitation.[12]

There will be a predictable, hostile reaction to facing up to 'the terrifying costs' of recognising reality. In not wanting to accept the limits of life on this planet, we begin to live a lie about ourselves and the world we inhabit. Indeed, Becker speaks of human character as a 'vital lie', based on denial, illusion and pretence.[13]

Ecological and cosmological perspectives can either expose this 'vital lie' of culture, or, by denying death in their respective ways, feed it with further self-deception. On the other hand, facing the reality of death leads to a deeper, more wonderful participation in the mystery of life. For genuine authenticity can be realised only through the courageous acceptance of creatureliness. In a more philosophical and religious range of reference, Becker writes: "By being or doing, we fashion something, an object or ourselves, and drop it into the confusion, make an offering of it, so to speak, to the life-force".[14] He is

---

11. Becker, *The Denial of Death*, 50.
12. Becker, *The Denial of Death*, 51.
13. Becker, *The Denial of Death*, 51.
14. Becker, *The Denial of Death*, 285.

calling us, in effect, to a lived sense of relationality, and to the virtues of praise and thankfulness that are at the heart of religious faith. Yet a shared sense of the human condition promises renewed collaboration between science and religion. Science improperly absorbs all truth into itself while downplaying the role of religion to stand for a larger version of truth. For its part, religious faith enables human beings,

> to wait in a condition of openness toward miracle and mystery, in the lived truth of creation, which would make it easier to survive and be redeemed because men would be less driven to undo themselves and would be more like the image which pleases their creator: awe-filled creatures trying to live in harmony with the rest of creation. Today we would add . . . they would be less likely to poison the rest of creation.[15]

Faith, then, has a contemplative dimension in its reverent openness to the mystery of creation and the Creator. Likewise, it exercises a redemptive effect in causing human beings to be less driven to self-destruct, and more disposed to realise the divine image in the works of love and justice. More to the point, the religious sense of the Creator and creation is of ecological value in that it demands living in harmony with "the rest of creation", and lessens the likelihood of poisoning it. Most of all, a genuinely creaturely consciousness relativises the harmful effects of the 'denial of death'. To accept our puniness in the face of the overwhelming majesty of the universe, to become aware of the unspeakable miracle of even a single living being, and so, begin to waken to the chaotic depths of the immense, inconclusive drama of creation, this is to come to a point of healing.

Following Frederick Perls, Becker detects four protective layers structuring the neurotic, death-denying self. The first two layers are the mundane, everyday layers of cliché and role which affect most of our lives and provide the criterion of success measured in terms of the right image. It is undoubtedly a considerable achievement to break out of the image of the self as it is imposed and communicated by an individualistic and consumerist culture. But Becker points to more resistant and armoured areas of the self, what the rhetoric of the spiritual life would describe as the darkness of the intellect and the hardness of heart of those resisting grace :

---

15. Becker, *The Denial* of Death, 282.

> ... the third is the stiff one to penetrate: it is the impasse that covers
> our feelings of being empty and lost, the very feeling we try to banish
> in building up our character defences. Under this layer is the fourth
> and the most baffling one: the 'death' or fear-of-death layer; this ...
> is the layer of our true and basic animal anxieties, the terror that we
> carry around in our secret heart. Only when we explode this fourth
> layer ... do we get to the layer of what we might call our 'authentic
> self': what we really are without shame, without disguise, without de-
> fences against fear.[16]

The authentic self, therefore, is realised in connectedness and harmony with all creation. It might be fittingly termed the 'ecological'
or 'cosmic' self—that is, the *religious* self as described above, bonded
to the Creator and all creation—in contrast to the tiny scope of the
fear-driven, illusory self produced by the denial of death. In effect,
the true self is realised only by befriending the mortal character of
existence.

As a consequence, authenticity consists in regaining the attitude of
humility, a sense of radical finiteness proper to creatureliness.[17] The
great value of Becker's work for an ecological and Christian spirituality lies in its revaluation of humility, in the most original sense of the
word. 'Humility', comes from the Latin *humus*, meaning earth, soil,
dirt. It indicates an awareness of the existential fact that spiritual life is
earthed, grounded, bound up with the immense dynamism of nature
into whose processes we are each and all immersed. Hence, the ancient liturgical injunction on Ash Wednesday, as the ashes are traced
on the forehead in the sign of the Cross : *Memento homo quia pulvis es*
... : 'Remember, man, thou art but dust ...'. In the catalogue of moral
virtues, humility is a quality of freedom. It is shown in a radical decen-
tring of the self, in the recognition that all is given, and that existence
is a gift. In this respect, humility enables human consciousness to deal
honestly, creatively with the dread of death by recognising oneself as a
creature within the mystery of the vast and uncanny universe.

Thus, death is allowed to emerge from its subterranean place of
influence, no longer to sap our energies or drive us to the frenzy of illusory immortality-projects. Humility is a connective virtue, relating

---

16. Becker, *The Denial* of Death, 57.
17. Becker, *The Denial* of Death, 58. See also Andras Angyal, *Neurosis and Treatment: a Holistic Theory* (New York: Wiley, 1965), 260.

us to the whole, and immersing each and all in a wondrous universe of gifts and giving. If ecological virtue is to be more than posturing, the cultivation of humility as a basic attitude in regard to life and creation is an obvious imperative. For out of this humble acceptance of mortality can come the wisdom we need if we are to coexist on this planet as "our common home". Life remains a question, within an overwhelmingly uncanny universe. It is most clear that that none of us is the centre of that universe, for we have emerged out of a vast cosmic process, and are dying back into it. When we begin to ask about the true centre, the true lifeforce of this overwhelming universe, an acceptance of self as mortal and finite begins. With that, if not precisely adoration, at least surrender to the often unnamed, incomprehensible creative generosity at the origin of all being and life can be realised. Only a decentred self, conscious of its mortal limitation, can live from and for a larger mystery, and in an integral ecology.

Becker's phenomenology of the psychology of fear and denial deserves recognition in an integral ecology. He notably stresses the existential value of the moral virtue of humility in our human sense of the universe, along with the value of what we might call a 'kenotic' attitude of self-surrender in life and in death. To this degree, his approach is powerfully religious, and anticipates what we present below as 'death in Christ'. In the present context, Becker connects befriending death with living in harmony with all creation, while 'the denial of death' can lead to the poisoning of the environment.

Becker's reflection resembles the biblical connection of death to sin as a punishment. Death is shrouded in a darkness deeper than the inevitable termination of biological life. Death, Paul declares, is the "wages of sin" (Rom 6:23). The implication is that death is the consequence and manifestation of sin. Sin is basically alienation from God, and the refusal of communion with the Creator – and creation. It is the choice for one's self against all others. In this context, the seemingly natural fact of death becomes the carrier of a profound sense of rupture and guilt. It looms through life as 'the last enemy' (1 Cor 15:26).[18]

Human culture is infected with the bias of 'original sin'.[19] We are born into a world skewed away from its centre and disrupted in the communion that God intends. To the degree existence is self-

---

18. James Alison, *The Joy of Being Wrong. Original Sin Through Easter Eyes* (New York: Crossroad, 1998) is illuminating in this whole area.
19. Alison, *The Joy of Being Wrong*, is a basic reference.

centred, death is experienced as menacing and meaningless. Life and death are locked in an absurd conflict, with death assured of victory. The transcendent Otherness of God and the created otherness of our neighbour cannot but appear as a threat. Everything is subjected to the self-serving demands of a skewed human freedom. The more human existence is turned in on itself, the more it occupies a shrinking universe. As a result, human identity is formed in competitive self-assertion against the Other. In this respect, death is the deepest threat: "The wages of sin is death". Death holds no promise of life; it is the carrier of all that is meaningless and threatening to the life we have chosen and made.[20]

The idea of death as the wages of sin invites an application to environmental issues. Environmental destruction, brought about by human greed and carelessness regarding the loss of biodiversity, to say nothing of its lethal effect on the lives of the poor amounts to a planetary instance of what the sins of pride, greed and selfishness can lead to. As the next section, 'Death in Christ', will indicate, death experienced as the wages of sin invites a deeper appreciation of the death of Christ and of Christian participation in his death and resurrection. Even aside from conversion to Christ, illusions born of the denial of death cannot be total. Life contests the reign of death as total, for ordinary lives know sudden impulses of wonder, unnameable hope and the exhilaration of great loves, just as all are humbled before the strange grandeur of moral achievement. In such moments, there is an uncanny, death-resistant, 'more' in the experience of the mystic, the artist, the martyr, the prophet, the thinker, the scientist and the activist. There is an intimation of eternity in the making, of 'eternity coming to be as time's own mature fruit'.[21]

Here a brief comparison of Becker's *Denial of Death* with Boros' *Mysterium Mortis*[22] is useful. Located in a classical philosophical and spiritual tradition, Boros' approach takes up where Becker's ends. He concedes that, empirically speaking, death implies dissolution and destruction. But Boros is intent on asking 'whether the complete re-

---

20. Karl Rahner, *On the Theology of Death*, Translated by CH Henkey (New York: Herder & Herder, 1962), 32–51.
21. See Peter C Phan, *Eternity in Time. A Study of Karl Rahner's Eschatology* (London: Associated University Press, 1988). 55. Also, 53–58; 207–210.
22. Ladislaus Boros, *The Moment of Truth: Mysterium Mortis*, translated by G Bainbridge (London: Burns and Oates, 1962).

moval from self which we undergo in death does not conceal a much more fundamental process which could be described . . . in terms of the progressive achievement of selfhood, of actively initiating the self to life.'[23] Like Becker, Boros purports to be exploring human consciousness. But instead of highlighting the strategies involved in the denial of death, Boros seeks to illumine the dynamics of self-transcendence discernible in actual living. A positive hermeneutics of mortality suggests that the thrust of human life is toward fulfillment—*in*, and even *through*, death. In dying, an individual existence moves to the bounds of its being. It awakes to a kind of full knowledge and liberty. The dynamics of personal existence that moved and motivated life in its normal course have been largely hidden from consciousness. At the moment of death, however, these surface into full awareness. Our deepest being is revealed as 'of unimaginable splendor', as the full dimensions of our being unfold.[24] In this respect, the self dies out of the limited individuality of the ego, into a more deeply relational form of being. This is to become aware of oneself as part of the universal whole, a new form of consciousness registering,

> . . . all at once and all together the universe that [the human person] has always borne hidden within himself, the universe with which he is already most intimately united, and which, one way or another, was always being produced from within him.[25]

The horizon in which this totality is experienced at the limits of our existence is now bounded only by the infinite mystery of God: 'Being flows toward [the person in death] like a boundless stream of things, meanings, persons and happenings, ready to convey him right into the Godhead'.[26] Death, therefore, is meeting with God. This limitless Other has been present in every stirring of our existence. It has been within us as our 'deepest mystery'. It has worked within all the elements and causes that have formed us, moving us towards an eternal destiny.[27] In the light of God, we are brought to a moment of final decision:

---

23. Boros, *The Moment of Truth*, viii. For elaboration, 1–23.
24. Boros, The Moment of Truth, viii. See 73–81.
25. Boros, The Moment of Truth, viii.
26. Boros, The Moment of Truth, viii.
27. Boros, *The Moment of Truth*, ix.

> There now man stands, free to accept or reject this splendor. In a last
> final decision, he either allows this flood of realities to flow past him,
> while he stands there eternally turned to stone, like a rock past which
> the life-giving stream flows on, noble enough in himself no doubt,
> but abandoned and eternally alone; or he allows himself to be carried
> along by this flood, becomes part of it and flows on to eternal fulfil-
> ment.[28]

Thus, Boros dramatically evokes the moment of decision when death
occurs as the final opportunity to crystallize one's life in a completely
personal act. Paradoxically, it is our most fully conscious and free
moment. It faces us with the decision – to choose life and the God
of life for whom we were made. Where Becker takes us back to the
psyche's primordial terror in the face of mortality, Boros bids us yield
to the movement of the human spirit anticipating its final homecom-
ing. All in all, art, mysticism, love and intelligence are promises that
are yet to be kept. In death, the self-transcending movement of our
existence will find its ultimate point of rest and its final vindication.[29]

As regards the concerns of this chapter, it would do violence to
history and to the achievement of a writer of great influence sixty
years ago, to expect any ecological application of his presentation of
the *mysterium mortis*. His concern is clearly the eschatological realisation of the self in the presence of God, and he does not deal with
how such a hope would affect the understanding of integral ecology
in the present. In this respect, Boros' brilliant analysis of the meaning of death is not incompatible with Becker's sense of creaturehood
and creation. Nonetheless, he does tend to give the impression that
in death the human spirit escapes this present world for the sake of
an eschatological fulfilment somewhat isolated from the universe of
God's creation of all things in Christ.

Both of the approaches of Becker and Boros we have summarily
sketched appeal to reasonably accessible levels of human experience.
Where Becker points to the repressed depths of consciousness, Boros
points to its heights. The one uncovers a primitive terror resulting
in the face of death; the other presents the thrust of life as somehow
positing death as the door to a final self-realisation. Psychologically
speaking, Becker's approach is more archeological. It searches into

---

28. Boros, *The Moment of Truth*, ix, and elaborated in 73–84.
29. See Phan, *Eternity in Time*, 75–115.

the psychic terror that affects culture with a 'denial of death'. Boros is more teleological in that it elucidates the movement of human existence in a manner best described as an affirmation or vindication of self-transcending consciousness.

At this point, we touch on a complex problem: How can hope find a psychological focus that is neither depressive nor schizophrenic? If it is morbid to constrict the whole hopeful direction of life to inevitable death, it would be just as evasive to repress the piercing tragedy at the heart of our existence. Facing death demands that we hold together both the negative and the positive dimensions of experience, even though these extremes never simply meet in any overall synthesis, even in an integral ecology. Here, the death of Christ crucified and risen recalls us to refocus our reflections on what faith reveals.

Death in Christ

Jacques Derrida's *The Gift of Death*[30] confronts his readers with the question of death, in a context formed by a number of major European thinkers: Kierkegaard, Heidegger, Levinas. He focuses on a writer little known in the English-speaking world, the Czech philosopher, Jan Patocka.[31] With Vaclev Havel, he authored *Charta 77* on human rights, and died of a brain haemorrhage after eleven hours of interrogation by the Czechoslovakian police during the Communist regime in 1977. For Patocka, the meaning of death was not only of deeply personal significance but also radically affected European culture and history. At the heart of that history, there is an abyss always resisting any totalising, theoretical solution or any reduction of human fate to the economy of exchange or reward. The dizzying excess of factual scientific knowledge characteristic of the West conceals the fact that there is no ever-ready answer to this question, unless it be given right in the 'black hole' of death itself. The task of historical responsibility is to be open to the possibility of such a gift which can be received only in faith. Authenticity at this point means a readiness to venture, beyond any knowledge or security, into absolute risk, so

---

30. Jacques Derrida, *The Gift of Death*, translated by David Wills (Chicago: The University of Chicago Press, 1995).
31. See Erazim Kohak, *Jan Patocka: Philosophy and Selected Writings* (Chicago: University of Chicago Press, 1989); and Jan Patocka, *Heretical Essays on the Philosophy of History* (Chicago: Open Court Publishing, 1995).

to enter into relationship with the transcendent Other, the God of selfless goodness, offered as a gift even in death itself.

In that venture, at that point of conversion, a new self is disclosed as the recipient of the gift, within the abyss in which history finds itself. True freedom is realised only in the waiting. Patocka observes,

> In the final analysis, the soul is not in relationship to an object, however elevated, such as the Platonic Good . . . which governs the ideal order of the Greek *polis* or the Roman *civitas*, but to a person who fixes it in his gaze while at the same time remaining beyond the reach of the gaze of the soul. As for knowing what that person is, such a question has not yet received an adequate thematic development within the perspective of Christianity.[32]

What, then, has theology been doing? In the risk of his own life, Patocka felt both an unsurpassable hope and a certain failure in Christian thought regarding the expression of the gift and the transcendent giver:

> Because of its foundation within the abyssal profundity of the soul, Christianity represents to this day the most powerful means—never yet superseded but not yet thought right through either—by which man is able to struggle against his own decline.[33]

Patocka's vision into the abyss in both history and the human spirit can provoke further reflection in today's experience of the destruction of the planetary environment and the ecological crisis that has ensued. Even here, we wait with him in this experience of death for the gift to continue be given in a consciousness transformed by Christian hope. Inspiring that transformation, there is an event which can allow both hope and failure to co-exist and illumine each another, namely, the crucifixion and death of Christ himself.[34] Christian meditation is not fixated on a skull, but on the cross of Jesus—which, in its deepest meaning, is a theophany. The all-creative mystery reveals itself through the cross as compassionate and transforming love. The death of Jesus was indeed deadly. It

---

32. As quoted in Derrida, *The Gift of Death*, 25.
33. Derrida, *The Gift of Death*, 28.
34. Gustave Martelet, *L'au-delà retrouvé. Christologie des fins dernières* (Paris: Desclée, 1975), 33-98.

occurred as failure, betrayal isolation, condemnation, torture and execution. God's love felt the force of the human problem of evil. However, the love that gave itself to the end (Jn 13:1) was not defeated by the power of evil.[35] For the death of the crucified Jesus enacts and embodies the ultimate form of life as he surrenders himself to the Father in solidarity with the defeated and the lost. With his existence concentrated in a final point of self-offering, God is self-revealed as a love stronger than death, as the creative mystery that upholds and fulfils all the best energies of life. To that degree, the crucified and risen One is the 'white hole' in the world of death. In Christ, crucified and risen, those receptive to the divine Gift are summoned to pass over from a self-serving existence into the realm of eternal life, already begun in faith, hope and love, the gifts that will last (1 Cor 13:13). Death, too, remains as the limit of this form of earthly life, but now transformed into an act of ultimate surrender to the Father in union with Christ, in yielding to the creativity of the Spirit who makes all things new. What is implied in death so understood is a participation in a larger vitality, and communion in an ultimate coexistence. The dissolution of death means rising to a new level of being, in the radiant space of Jesus' resurrection.[36] The entropy affecting each individual biological existence is dissipated to allow for a higher realisation of communion, in relationship to the "all" and participation in the whole.

The vector of self-transcendence in the direction of communion is underwritten, as it were, in the dynamics of the cosmos itself. The sense of self as a self-contained particle is revealed to be the wave of communion, the relational self. There is an upward vector of ascent from electron, to atoms, to molecules, to proteins, to cells, to organisms, to the complexity of the human brain, and to the cosmic overture of human consciousness. The direction of life is one of transformation in increasingly rich and complex relationships. Might not the notion of death be more hopefully and realistically located in such a process? In that context, death would not mean dissolution so much as the expansion of the self into its fullest rela-

---

35. See Anthony J Kelly and Francis F Moloney, *Experiencing God in the Gospel of John* (New York: Paulist Press, 2003), 270–286.
36. Denis Edwards, 'Resurrection and the Costs of Evolution: A Dialogue with Rahner on Non-Interventionist Theology', *Theological Studies* 67 (2006): 816–833—especially 827-833.

tionality. Death would not be an alien intruder, but a relative—'Sister Death' as St Francis could pray—within cosmic promise of the fullness of life in Christ.

It is true that the resurrection is not resuscitation to this present biological life, nor does it entail a relocation in the time and space of this world. It is no cure for death. Only a transformation of our whole embodied existence can answer the hopes written into life. By participating in his rising from the tomb, the entropy and limiting individuality of biological life, is definitively overcome. In him a new creation is anticipated when Christ is given as 'the resurrection and the life' (Jn 11:25). The particular realism of this new creation is expressed in all four Gospel narratives in regard to the empty tomb. It is the historical marker of the cosmic transformation that has begun in Christ:[37] 'So if anyone is in Christ, there is a new creation: everything old has passed away; see, everything has become new!' (2 Cor 5:17).

Hope, nonetheless, remains hope. It lives always in the in-between of what is, and what is yet to be, as it waits on the mystery of final transformation. Even the New Testament writer soberly concedes, 'As it is, we do not yet see everything in subjection to him' (Heb 2: 8f). Yet for all the sobriety of Christian hope, the great conviction is remains firm. In Christ, the universe has been changed. Death has been radically 'Christened'. Christ did not die out of the world, but into it, to become its innermost coherence and dynamism. Indeed, in his death, resurrection and ascension, the mystery of the incarnation is complete. For the Christian, dying in Christ is to surrender to the transforming power of such a resurrection, is to be newly embodied in the future form of the cosmos itself:[38]

> The last enemy to be destroyed is death . . . When all things are subjected to him, the Son himself will also be subjected to him who put all things under him, that God may be all in all (1 Cor 15: 26–28).

All mortal existence is poised, therefore, over an abyss of life. The empty tomb, a sign of the creative power of the Spirit, is of cosmic

---

37. On the empty tomb, see Anthony J Kelly, *The Resurrection Effect: Transforming Christian Life and Thought* (Maryknoll NY: Orbis, 2008),139–145.
38. For elaboration of this point, see Denis Edwards, *Jesus and the Cosmos* (New York: Paulist Press, 1991), 103–132.

significance.[39] It suggests the full-bodied reality of resurrection, and seeds history with questions and wonder as to what great transformation is afoot. The empty tomb, so soberly recorded in each of the four Gospels, offers no salvation in mere emptiness. It functions as a factor within the awakening of faith, as a new consciousness of life unfolds. It moves first from the empty tomb, discovered as a puzzling fact. It awakens to cosmic surprise over what had happened, for Jesus appears as newly and wonderfully alive: 'Do not be afraid. I am the first and the last, and the living one. I was dead, and see, I am alive forever and ever' (Rev 1:17–18). Then faith returns to the tomb as an emblem of the new creation. From there it expands into the limitless horizons of a transformation of all things in Christ. Such faith is not primarily looking back at a death, but facing forward into the promise of eternal life, in a universe transformed.

Before the Foundation of the World

In the meantime we are confronted with the agony of the world and the cost of evolution, with its deaths, extinctions, violence and dead ends: "the whole of creation has been has been groaning in labor pains until now" (Rom 8:23). Note, for instance, the extinction of the eighty thousand extraordinarily complex creatures of the Cambrian period, unearthed in the Burgess Shale in British Columbia.[40] Side by side with the cosmic cooperation that enables the evolutionary process, 'competition, pain, and death (are) intrinsic to evolutionary processes'.[41] In the agony and struggle inscribed in nature itself, we turn to the image of 'the Lamb that was slaughtered before the foundation of the world' (Rev 13:8; see also Rev, 5:6, 11–12; 7:13–17; 12:11). This image suggests that there is an aboriginally self-giving divine love constitutive of the creation and providence. Without such a perspective, human and evolutionary history could lead to a blank wall of hopelessness. The self-giving love of God constitutive

---

39. John Polkinghorne, *Science and Creation. The Search for Understanding* (London: SPCK, 1988) 64-68.

40. For an abundance of documentation and marvellous instances of fossil remains, see Stephen Jay Goulding, *Wonderful Life. The Burgess Shale and the Nature of History* (London: Penguin, 1989).

41. Denis Edwards, *Partaking of God: Trinity, Evolution and Ecology* (Collegeville, MN: Liturgical Press), 88; further, 130–46, where Edwards discusses 'Evolution, Cooperation, and the Theology of Original Sin'.

of creation is expressed in several places in the New Testament. Paul affirms that Christ Jesus emptied himself of 'the form of God', to take on the form of a slave (Phil 2:5–7).[42] In post-Pauline developments, the author of the Letter to the Colossians describes the Christ as 'the image of the invisible God, the first born of all creation . . . He himself is before all things, and in him all things hold together' (Col 1:15, 17). Similarly, the Letter to the Ephesians proclaims: 'He chose us in him before the foundation of the world to be holy and blameless before him in love' (Eph 1:4). Then, at the foundation of Johannine Christology is the intimate union between the *Logos* with God that pre-existed 'the beginning' (John 1:1–2). In his final prayer, the Johannine Jesus prays to his Father that he might return to the glory which was his in God's presence 'before the world existed' (Jn 17:5).[43]

Completing and intensifying this perspective of God's original, pre-existent and sacrificial is the vision of the slaughtered and risen lamb shining into all the darkness and violence of history, 'from the foundation of the world' (Rev 5:6; 13:8). This light must be taken to penetrate even into the evolutionary *agōnia* of the cosmos.,[44] for suffering and death are a necessary part of the evolutionary process.[45] The realism of faith in the Crucified cannot hide from the agony of the Cross, nor fail to relate it to the suffering and dying inherent in an evolutionary universe within this planetary environment. The au-

---

42. For a convincing exegetical and theological argument in favour of pre-existence, see Brendan Byrne, 'Christ's Pre-Existence in Pauline Soteriology', in *Theological Studies* 58 (1997): 308–30.

43. The incarnate *Logos*, known as 'Jesus Christ' (Jn 1:14–17), is the key to the mystery of the Johannine Jesus.

44. Revelation's presentation of the sheer grace of Jesus' death and resurrection 'from before all time', in a way parallel to the Pauline understanding of Jesus as the image of an invisible God (Philippians and Colossians), and the Johannine understanding of the eternal union between God and the *Logos*, may prove to be a significant contribution to Christian ecological thought.

45. Most Christian theologians correctly have recourse to the unlimited love of God, manifested in the unconditional free-gift of Jesus Christ, allowing the cosmos to run its course freely. See survey of approaches in Catherine Vincie, *Worship and the New Cosmology* (Collegeville, MN: Liturgical Press, 2014), 43–80 where she surveys a number of scholars who attempt to respond to the problem of the agony of the cosmos (John Haught, Denis Edwards, Arthur Peacocke, Elizabeth Johnson, Ilia Delio). The pre-existent slain and risen Lamb can surely be part of such a suggestion.

thor of Revelation locates Jesus' sacrifice for the sins of the world as primordial, as 'before the foundation of the world'. That is to suggest that the failures and ambiguities of creation that have occurred from the beginnings of time can be already washed clean by the blood of the Lamb (Rev 7:13–17). The key element in the relationship of God to the world, that is—from 'before the foundation of the world'—has been the continuing presence of the crucified and risen One: 'Do not be afraid; I am the first and the last, and the living one. I was dead, and see, I am alive forever and ever; and I have the keys of Death and Hades' (Rev. 1:17b–18). Regarding the violence, pain, suffering and death marking human history and the ecology of the planet, Moloney remarks,

> John the Seer introduces the crucified into that process, bringing God's healing, in and through his pre-existent Son, a Lamb slain before all time. Thus, that community faces its ambiguous reality with a hope founded in awareness that it has been cleansed by the blood of the slain Lamb since 'before the foundation of the world'.[46]

The New Testament addresses the mystery of pain, suffering. death, and human failure without hesitation, and in the light of the death, burial and resurrection of Jesus (see 1 Cor 15:3–19). In that light we accept this planetary existence and our responsibilities within it. Without this backdrop of a divine self-sacrificial love, the ecology of the planet can seem like a dismal obituary. The past, if recalled at all, is a catalogue of suffering, violence and death. An integral ecology must learn from the ecological sciences to appreciate the varied wonder of life, to mourn the extinctions that have occurred, and to

---

46. Francis J Moloney, SDB, 'The Gospel of Creation: A Biblical Response to *Laudato Si'* (A Paper given in October, 2015, in Rome, at the ACU-CUA Centre during a Conference on 'the Greening of the Church' [soon to be published]. I am here following the work of outstanding scholars such as Moloney and Eugenio Corsini. The Book of Revelation deals with the perennial revelation of God's saving activity in the death and resurrection of Jesus 'from the foundation of the world'. See Eugenio Corsini, *The Apocalypse: The Perennial Revelation of Jesus Christ*, trans. Francis J Moloney, Good News Studies 5 (Wilmington, DE: Michael Glazier, 1983) and *Apocalisse di Gesù secondo Giovanni* (Torino: Società Editrice, Internazionale, 2002). For a summary of his argument, see Moloney, *Reading the New Testament in the Church*, 180–89. The most exhaustive contemporary commentary on Revelation in English is David E Aune, *Revelation*, Word Biblical Commentary 52a–52c (Dallas, TX: Word, 1997–1998).

lament over the lethal presence in the environment of human society and culture. But any conclusion based only on the violence, failure and death intrinsic to the evolution of life on earth, would be premature without the special energies of Christian hope. For this hope breathes a limitless self-sacrificial love on the part of God, creating the universe, and guiding it in a providence leading to transformation.

The Realm of Otherness

Now, given that Christian theology informing integral ecology is committed to the paschal realism of Christ's death and resurrection, it offers no super theory explaining death and blunting the edge of hope. In this consideration of the ecological dimension of death, questions remain. The first is a theological embarrassment. Is our theology sufficiently humble? There can be no theological theory or ecological system that masters death, nor any egomaniac subjectivity appropriating death to its purposes. Inscribed into the course of our lives, there is an elemental rupture; and any expression of hope that represses the lethal force of death is not starting from scratch. Consoling themselves with a beauteous sense of nature, some may aspire to a form of ecological immortality in which nothing really dies. Others may take refuge in the wonder of the universe unfolding through its billions of years in the hope of attaining some kind of cosmic immortality impervious to the finality of death. Even theologians, evading the brute fact of death, may find ourselves offering a guided tour of the world of eschatological fulfilment so as to give the impression of being already ensconced in glory. Still, it remains, with whatever humility it can summon before the awful gift of existence, that theology is continually challenged to catch up with a Becker or a Patocka and with the martyrs who have died in apparent defeat. How does theology inform an integral ecology, and, in the words of Becker, enable human beings to 'wait in a condition of openness toward miracle and mystery, in the lived truth of creation'?[47]

In a more Levinasian mode, one might suggest that 'being-toward-death' progressively brings to human consciousness the uncanny otherness to which we are beholden. The face of the suffering other—even as environmentally understood—precedes ethical theory and ecological sensibility, to give us to ourselves in moral

---

47. Becker, *The Denial of Death*, 282.

responsibility. The human person is not a pure, open-ended, undecided subjectivity enfolding everything into itself. It is a self consti-
tutionally beholden to the other in its disconcerting strangeness and
claim. A form of reason proper to an idealised, independent rational
ego here yields to an affective surrender to the *who* and *what* of the
other—which abstract reason often obstructs. If life leads to personal
responsibility in this way, the deaths of others—and the deaths and
diminishment occurring in nature itself—draw consciousness to an
inexpressible limit—to the end of self-contained independence and
to the edge of the utterly other. To die is finally to face that original
Other, hitherto only partially disclosed in all others who have had a
claim on our lives, especially in their suffering. In that event, we are
left only with the possibility of an ultimate surrender to this 'Other',
for the sake of others, as in the cross of Jesus, and in the self-offering that Becker refers to above. The grain of wheat falling into the
ground does not remain alone. The death of others, either of our fellow humans or of life-forms in the environment, strikes deep. In the
'sublime communion' of life as the gift of God [89], we 'mean the
world' to one another. And when death removes that other and reduces communication to silence, we feel that a world ends and that
the dark otherness of reality comes close.

The question persists, despite the virtuosity of transcendental
analysis: has the notion of self-transcendence gone far enough? To
put it another way, are we really letting ourselves and others, actually
die? In consequence, theology may have been all too timid regarding
the social meaning of death as the final breaking down of self-contained individual existence. All that remains in a new creation in
Christ is relationship to, and responsibility for, the other, for the sake
of 'a sublime communion' in God, the ultimate other in all others? (1
Cor 15:28).

In its concentration on the salvific efficacy of the death of Christ,
theology may be too inclined to hurry past the caesura of Holy Saturday, so graphically portrayed in the stripped altars and emptiness
of the tabernacle. Before death means resurrection, it means being
dead, descending into the realm of the dead, as when, in the words of
the Apostles Creed, Jesus 'descended into hell'—crucified, dead and
buried. Whatever Christian hope is, it is not a video replay of highlights once our team has won. Here theology must pause if it is to address the inevitable reservations associated with unconditional hope.

In Holy Saturday, a healing providence makes time for all our human griefs and lamentations, in a world of apparent God-forsakenness, failure, and waiting for God to act in God's good time, in God's own way. Jesus was not only dead, but buried. In failure, condemnation and suffering, he has gone down to the depths of universal dread. At this point, we may ask, is it possible to hurry past the deadly reality of the cross to a kind of automatic resurrection? That would obscure the fact that there is a time, in history and consciousness, before that Friday can be affirmed as 'Good' and that Saturday as 'Holy'. The paschal mystery of the Three Holy Days is a complex symbol in the experience of violence and death. Only by waiting on that complexity can the imagination be christened, and hope expand beyond repressive optimism to its authentically theological character.[48]

The horizon of faith is shaped by Christ's self-giving unto death for the sake of the world's salvation. This gift occurs so that 'by the grace of God, he might taste death for everyone' (Heb 2:9). Even more specifically, Christ is sent 'so that he might . . . free those who all their lives were held in slavery by the fear of death' (Heb 2:14–15). In the gift of Christ, a multi-dimensioned giving is at work. Christ gives himself in death for the salvation of the world. This looks back to the Father giving the Son into such a death. In the power of the Spirit, this death becomes a gift given into the dark abyss of the death of each Christian: 'Those who believe in me, even though they die, they will live' (Jn 11:25). The realm of death is not annihilation or ultimate isolation. It is included in the way of the Son reaching into the darkest of human depths. The point most distant from life and from God is reached only by self-giving love, for the dark abyss of death is not outside the reach of the divine giver.[49] Nature is not the all-encompassing totality, for that is found only in the gift of God that heals and transforms all that nature is. Nor is this gift simply identified with the dynamics of spiritual desire and aspiration. The *eros* of the human spirit, even when it looks beyond this world, does not hold within its grasp what can only be divinely given. Christian hope opens itself to receive the gift of the One who 'loved his own unto the end' (Jn 13:1). Jesus' self-offering in death is given as the form and energy of true life: 'We

---

48. See Anthony J Kelly, *Eschatology and Hope* (Maryknoll, NY: Orbis,2006), especially chapter 4, 'The Paschal Mystery: the Parable of Hope', 73–95.

49. See Kelly and Moloney, *Experiencing God in the Gospel of John*, especially Chapter 11, 'The God of Life in the World of Death', 238–250.

know love by this, that he laid down his life for us—and we ought lay
down our lives for one another' (1 Jn 3:16). Paul, with his vivid awareness of this new order of grace, asks, 'He who did not withhold his
own Son, but gave him up for all of us, will he not with him also give
us everything else?' (Rom 8:32). He goes on to proclaim that 'neither
death nor life . . . nor things present nor things to come . . . nor height
nor depth, nor anything else in all creation, will be able to separate us
from the love of God in Christ Jesus, our Lord' (Rom 8:37–39).

When hope awakens to the universe of grace, all existence is laid
open to the transforming power of the gift disclosed in the Cross
of Jesus. The more hope moves toward it, the more the lower and
upper limits of the mystery of death are intensified. The crucifixion
of Jesus was experienced by his first followers as the defeat of all he
was and stood for. He was condemned, tortured, executed, died and
was buried. But now, in the light of his resurrection, Christian hope
is sustained by the witness of these same early disciples. He appeared
to them in the radiance of another life, as the conqueror of sin and
death. Both the lower and upper limits of hope are extended. Theology, focused on the revelatory event of the death of Christ, holds
together two seemingly conflicting vectors of experience. The saving
mystery of this death reaches deeper than any death we know. Jesus,
in 'tasting death for everyone', tastes the extent of evil, isolation and
rejection, the full weight of the sins of the world. His death reaches
higher than anything life might naturally aspire to, namely, sharing
in the deathless life of God. The crucified and living one embodies
the ultimate life form: 'I am the first and the last, and the living one. I
was dead, and see, I am alive forever and ever; and I have the keys of
Death and Hades' (Rev 1:18).

Though hope relies on the God whose love is stronger than death,
it has the realism to admit that 'in the days of his flesh, Jesus offered
up prayers and supplications, with loud cries and tears to him who
was able to save him from death' (Heb 5:7). The God of life has acted.
The Father did not save Jesus from death, but vindicated and glorified him in his death, by raising him to a new order of life. As the
form and source of new life, he is the firstborn from the dead (Col
1:18). The same realism contemplates his risen body marked forever
by the wounds of the Cross. He bears forever the marks of his solidarity in suffering what most terrifies and defeats mortal beings: 'by his
wounds you have been healed' (1 Pet 2:25). In the light of his death,

hope looks through death and beyond it. But it does so first of all by being a way into it—in union with Christ in his death: 'Since therefore the children share in flesh and blood, he himself likewise partook of the same nature, that, through death, he might destroy him who has the power of death' (Heb 2:14–18). To be united with him in his death is to share his victory over all the demonic forces that work in human culture—and, consequently, in the environment, through the threat of death. By sharing in his death, hope is already sharing in his resurrection (Rom 6:3–5). Still, hope remains hope. It is never immune from the darkness of life. It must show its own patience. It means waiting for the whole mystery of love to prove itself stronger than death and all the demonic powers that use the threat of death for their purposes. The New Testament expresses a sober realism:

> As it is, we do not yet see everything in subjection to them. But we see Jesus who for a little while was made lower than the angels, crowned with glory and honour because of the suffering of death so that by the grace of God he might taste death for everyone (Heb 2:8–9).

There is a further edge at which theology trembles: the mystery of God. Though the holy and immortal God does not die, there something about the way God is God, about the way the Trinity is these three self-giving divine persons, which leads death into the deepest darkness of all. This deeper darkness is not a threat, but an intimation of life in its Trinitarian and most vital dimensions. Union with Christ in his death is most radically self-abandonment to the Father. It yields to the incalculable creativity of the life-giving Spirit. It means incorporation in the Body of Christ. In this Trinitarian frame of reference, a self-surrender is inevitably asked of each mortal being. But that is to share in the unreserved self-emptying of the divine three in relation to each other, and to the world which they have created and drawn into their communal life. Death, in this respect, is the last, and perhaps the only truly genuine act of adoration of the God whose life is self-giving love. Only by dying out of the cultural and biological systems and projects structuring this present existence, are human beings remade in conformity with the self-giving and communal trinitarian life of God. As Ghislain Lafont points out,[50] dying

---

50. Ghislain Lafont, *Peut-on connaître Dieu en Jésus-Christ?* (Paris: Cerf, 1969), 237–258. For the broader context, see Anne Hunt, *The Trinity and the Paschal*

in Christ means a recentering of our existence along truly personal lines. Autonomous existence within the world yields to unbroken life of communion with God, and with all in God. In conclusion, we hope to have shown a consideration of death makes for a more integral ecology, and how such an integral ecology makes for a deeper understanding of "Sister Death".

Mystery: A Development in Recent Catholic Theology (Collegeville, MN: The Liturgical Press, 1997), Chapter 2, 'Death and Being, Human and Divinity', 37–56. In regard to eschatology, see Hunt, chapter 11, 'Trinity and Eschatology', in *The Trinity: Nexus of the Mysteries of Faith* (Maryknoll, NY: Orbis, 2005), 200–216.

Contributors

Frank Brennan SJ is Chief Executive Officer of Catholic Social Services Australia. At the time of writing this paper he was a Professor of Law at Australian Catholic University Adjunct Professor at the ANU College of Law and National Centre for Indigenous Studies and a Fellow at the Australian Centre for Christianity and Culture, Canberra. His recent publications include: *Amplifying that still, Small Voice : A Collection of* and *No Small Change: The Road to Recognition for Indigenous Australia.*

John Capper is Director of Learning and Teaching for the University of Divinity. He has exercised leadership in theology teaching since 1989. His PhD is from the University of Cambridge, for a dissertation on Karl Barth's theology of joy. John is an ordained Anglican and contributes to the educational offerings and professional development of the University and to academic governance of a number of institutions.

Bruce Duncan CSsR studied economics and political science at the University of Sydney. During this time he was one of the founding editors of *National Outlook* magazine. Since 1986 he has taught at Yarra Theological Union, Melbourne, and coordinates the program in social justice studies. He was a member of the Melbourne Catholic Commission for Justice, Development and Peace (1994–2007), and a consultant with Catholic Social Services Victoria (1998–2007). He is one of the founders of the advocacy organisation, Social Policy Connections, and of the Yarra Institute for Religion and Social Policy, of which he is the Director.

Norm Habel is currently Professorial Fellow at Flinders University, Adelaide, previously he was professor of Biblical Studies in the USA from 1960–1973. In 1974 he returned to Australia and established the first Religion Studies Department in Australia. From 1984–87 he was Principal of Kodaikanal International School in South India. He has long been involved in issues of biblical interpretation and social justice. His research includes *The Earth Bible*, a five volume international project with other scholars reading the Bible from the perspective of justice for Earth. A sequel to these volumes is the *Earth Bible Commentary* series which was launched in 2011, the first volume of which is his work entitled: *The Birth, the Curse and the Greening of Earth.*

His latest publications are entitled *Exploring Ecological Hermeneutics, An Inconvenient Text* and *A Rainbow of Mysteries.*

Peter MJ Hess is a Catholic theologian specialising in issues at the interface between science and religion, particularly in the areas of evolution, sustainability, and climate change. With an MA from Oxford University and a PhD from the Graduate Theological Union (Berkeley), he is co-author of *Catholicism and Science* (Greenwood, 2008), and of various articles and book chapters on sustainability. Peter Hess has taught on the adjunct faculties of the University of San Francisco and Dominican University of California. He is a fellow of the International Society for Science and Religion, the American Scientific Affiliation, and the International Big History Association

Anthony Kelly CSsR undertook doctoral and post-doctoral studies in Rome, Toronto and Paris. For many years he was involved in the Yarra Theological Union in Melbourne. President of *YTU* for ten years. Formerly President of Australian Catholic Theological Association. Past Chair of the Forum of Australian Catholic Institutes of Theology. He was the head of Sub-Faculty of Philosophy and Theology at the Australian Catholic University from 1999–2004. In February 2004, Anthony Kelly was appointed by Pope John Paul II to the International Theological Commission. His recent publications include: *Upward: Faith, Church and Ascension of Christ*, and *Laudato Si': An Integral Ecology and the Catholic Vision.*

Abigail L Lofte is a PhD candidate in the Faculty of Theology at the University of Saint Michael's College. Her research focuses on the intersection of Thomas Berry's ecotheology and Edward Schillebeeckx's resurrectional theology to create an ecotheological anthropology that takes seriously the resurrection of Jesus as the impetus for establishing mutually enhancing relationships between humans and Earth. Expanding the vision of mission from that of the first-century disciples, her theology seeks to reinvigorate communities to work for renewal of the world through care for the Earth.

Ted Peters is Research Professor Emeritus of Systematic Theology and Ethics at Pacific Lutheran Theological Seminary and the Graduate Theological Union in Berkeley, California, and co-editor with Robert John Russell of the journal, *Theology and Science,* at the Center for Theology and the Natural Sciences. He serves on the Standards Working Group (SWG) of the California Institute of Regenerative Medicine (CIRM), which sets standards for stem cell line derivation, oocyte donation, and related practices. His current area of research centres on astro-theology: cosmology and the questions of God.

Marie Turner is an Adjunct Senior Lecturer in Biblical Studies in the Flinders University Department of Theology. Her work focusses on Old Testament and the Pauline Letters of the New Testament. Chiefly interested in the wisdom literature of the Bible, including the Deutero-canonical books, and the historical books. Expertise in deconstructive and ecological readings. For several years she as involved in the Earth Bible Project and the new Ecological Commentary series. Her publications include: *A Friendly Guide to the Old Testament,* and *God's Wisdom or the Devil's Envy: Death and Creation Deconstructing in the Wisdom of Solomon.* She is a Past President of the Australian Catholic Biblical Association.

CPSIA information can be obtained
at www.ICGtesting.com
Printed in the USA
BVHW072037301219
568186BV00001B/46/P